MYSTERIES OF ROME

33 HIDDEN STORIES FROM A SACRED CITY

DAVID PETAULT

CONTENTS

FOREWORD

I am happy you chose to read "Mysteries of Rome." It's a collection of short stories, mysteries, and folklore from one of my favorite cities in the world. I hope these tales will help you capture the essence of Rome, from its ancient legends to its enduring mysteries.

Each story offers a unique glimpse into the people, places, and events that make Rome so captivating.

Whether you're a history enthusiast or just love a good story, I hope you enjoy exploring the magic of Rome through these pages as much as I enjoyed gathering the stories and writing them.

David Petault

A BRIEF HISTORY OF ROME

Rome's legendary foundation is dated to 753 BCE, attributed to Romulus and Remus, twin sons of Mars, the god of war. Raised by a she-wolf, the brothers grew up to found Rome. After a quarrel, Romulus killed Remus and became the first king of Rome. This mythical origin marks the beginning of the Roman Kingdom, a period of consolidation and early expansion. The city was initially a small settlement of Latin tribes on the Palatine Hill. Over time, Rome incorporated surrounding areas through alliances and conquests, growing its influence and population.

In 509 BCE, the last Roman king, Tarquin the Proud, was overthrown, and the Roman Republic was established. The Republic was characterized by a complex system of checks and balances, with power divided among elected officials and advisory bodies, including the Senate. The early Republic faced numerous challenges, including social class conflicts between the patricians (aristocratic families) and the plebeians (common citizens). These struggles led to the creation of the Twelve Tables, Rome's first set of written laws, which aimed to balance the interests of both classes. Rome's expansion during the Republic was marked by the Punic Wars (264-146 BCE) against Carthage. The most famous Carthaginian general, Hannibal, led a daring invasion of Italy, but Rome ultimately emerged victorious, establishing itself as a dominant Mediterranean power.

The late Republic was a period of internal turmoil and civil wars. Key figures such as Julius Caesar, Pompey, and Crassus formed the First Triumvirate, a political alliance that dominated Roman politics. However, the alliance eventually disintegrated, leading to a power struggle. Julius Caesar's crossing of the Rubicon River in 49 BCE marked the beginning of a civil war between Caesar and Pompey. Caesar's victory and subsequent appointment as dictator for life in 44 BCE signaled the end of the Roman Republic. His assassination on the Ides of March in 44 BCE led to another round of civil wars. The Second Triumvirate, consisting of Octavian (later Augustus), Mark Antony, and Lepidus, was formed to avenge Caesar's death. However, internal conflicts led to the defeat of Antony and Cleopatra at the Battle of Actium in 31 BCE.

Octavian emerged as the sole ruler of Rome, marking the transition to the Roman Empire.

In 27 BCE, Octavian was granted the title Augustus, becoming the first Roman emperor. His reign ushered in a period of relative peace and stability known as the Pax Romana (Roman Peace), which lasted for over two centuries. Augustus implemented numerous reforms, including the reorganization of the military and the establishment of a professional bureaucracy. The Roman Empire expanded significantly during the early centuries, reaching its greatest territorial extent under Emperor Trajan (98-117 CE). Rome's provinces stretched from Britain to the Middle East, incorporating diverse cultures and peoples. However, the empire also faced numerous challenges. The Crisis of the Third Century (235-284 CE) was a period of political instability, economic decline, and external invasions. The empire was temporarily stabilized under Emperor Diocletian, who implemented administrative reforms and divided the empire into the Western and Eastern Roman Empires.

The Western Roman Empire faced increasing pressure from barbarian invasions, economic difficulties, and internal strife. In 410 CE, the Visigoths, led by Alaric, sacked Rome, dealing a significant blow to the empire's prestige and stability. The final collapse of the Western Roman Empire is traditionally dated to 476 CE, when the last Roman emperor, Romulus Augustulus, was deposed by the Germanic chieftain Odoacer. This event marked the end of ancient Rome and the beginning of the Middle Ages in Western Europe. While the Western Roman Empire fell, the Eastern Roman Empire, known as the Byzantine Empire, continued to thrive. Founded by Emperor Constantine the Great, who moved the capital to Byzantium (renamed Constantinople), the Byzantine Empire preserved Roman traditions and governance.

The Byzantine Empire reached its zenith under Emperor Justinian I (527-565 CE), who sought to reconquer lost western territories and codified Roman law in the Corpus Juris Civilis. The empire played a crucial role in preserving classical knowledge and influencing the development of medieval Europe. However, the Byzantine Empire faced its own challenges, including invasions by Persians, Arabs, and later the Seljuk Turks. The Fourth Crusade in 1204 resulted in the sack of Constantinople, further weakening the empire. The Byzantine Empire ultimately fell to the Ottoman Turks in 1453, marking the end of Roman continuity and the beginning of the Ottoman Empire.

Rome's legacy is profound and far-reaching. Roman law, political institutions, and cultural achievements have left an indelible mark on Western civilization. The concept of republican governance influenced the development of modern democratic systems, while Roman engineering and architecture set standards for infrastructure and urban planning. Latin, the language of Rome, became the foundation for the Romance languages and a vital component of scientific and legal terminology. Roman literature, philosophy, and art continue to be studied and revered for their contributions to human thought and culture. Christianity, which emerged within the Roman Empire, became the dominant religion of the empire and subsequently of Europe. The Catholic Church, centered in Rome, played a pivotal role in preserving Roman heritage and shaping the medieval and modern worlds.

The Renaissance period, beginning in the 14th century, saw a revival of interest in classical antiquity, with Rome as a central source of inspiration. This era was marked by significant advancements in art, science, and humanism, with artists such as Michelangelo and Raphael drawing heavily from Roman ideals. The city of Rome itself underwent extensive architectural and cultural revitalization, becoming a hub for artists, scholars, and the intellectual elite.

In the modern era, Rome became the capital of the unified Kingdom of Italy in 1871. This period saw Rome's transformation into a modern city, with the construction of new infrastructure, government buildings, and public services. The city played a crucial role during World War II, experiencing both the impact of Fascist rule under Mussolini and the Allied liberation.

Post-war Rome experienced rapid growth and development, becoming a vibrant metropolis and a symbol of Italian culture and heritage. The city hosted the 1960 Summer Olympics, which further boosted its international standing. Today, Rome is a bustling capital, home to significant political, cultural, and religious institutions, including the Italian government and the Vatican City.

Rome's rich history is preserved in its countless historical sites, museums, and cultural landmarks. The Colosseum, the Roman Forum, the Pantheon, and the Vatican Museums are just a few examples of the city's unparalleled historical and architectural heritage. The Eternal City continues to attract millions of visitors each year, drawn by its unique blend of ancient history and modern vitality.

Rome's history, from its mythical beginnings through its rise and fall as a powerful empire, to its enduring legacy in modern times, is a testament to its profound influence on the development of Western civilization. The city's contributions to law, governance, language, art, and religion have left an indelible mark on human history, making Rome a timeless symbol of cultural and historical significance.

MYSTERIES OF ROME

$$1$$

THE MYSTERIOUS DISAPPEARANCE
OF ROMULUS

The story of Romulus, the legendary founder of Rome, begins in the 8th century BCE. According to Roman tradition, Romulus and his twin brother Remus were born to Rhea Silvia, daughter of Numitor, the rightful king of Alba Longa. Numitor had been deposed by his brother Amulius, who forced Rhea Silvia to become a Vestal Virgin to prevent her from having children who could claim the throne.

Despite Amulius's precautions, Rhea Silvia conceived twins, allegedly by the god Mars. Upon discovering her pregnancy, Amulius imprisoned Rhea Silvia and ordered the infants to be drowned in the Tiber River. However, the servant tasked with this deed took pity on the babies and placed them in a basket, setting it adrift on the river.

. . .

The basket came ashore at the site of the future Rome. According to legend, a she-wolf found the twins and suckled them. Eventually, a shepherd named Faustulus discovered the boys and raised them with his wife, Acca Larentia.

As young men, Romulus and Remus learned of their true identity and lineage. They gathered a group of supporters and returned to Alba Longa, where they killed Amulius and restored their grandfather Numitor to the throne.

The twins then decided to found a new city. They chose a site along the Tiber River, but disagreed on which hill to build it on - Romulus favored the Palatine Hill, while Remus preferred the Aventine Hill. They agreed to settle the dispute through augury, a method of divination. Each brother stood on his chosen hill and waited for a sign from the gods in the form of birds. Remus saw six vultures, but Romulus claimed to have seen twelve.

The augury led to a quarrel, during which Romulus killed Remus. There are varying accounts of this event. Some sources suggest Remus mockingly jumped over the low walls Romulus had started to build, prompting Romulus to kill him in anger. Others portray it as a calculated act to eliminate a rival.

With Remus gone, Romulus proceeded to found the city on the Palatine Hill. According to Roman historians, this occurred on April 21, 753 BCE, a date celebrated in Rome as the city's birthday.

Romulus implemented several measures to populate and organize his new city. He opened Rome as an asylum for fugitives, exiles, and other outcasts, rapidly increasing the population. He divided the people into three tribes: the Ramnes (possibly named after Romulus himself), the Tities (possibly named after the Sabine king Titus Tatius), and the Luceres (origin unclear, possibly Etruscan).

To address the shortage of women in Rome, Romulus organized a festival and invited the neighboring Sabines. During the festivities, the Romans abducted many Sabine women, an event known as the "Rape of the Sabine Women" (the term "rape" here meaning "abduction" rather than sexual assault).

· · ·

This act led to war with the Sabines. The conflict ended when the Sabine women, now married to Romans and with children, intervened to reconcile the two sides. As part of the peace agreement, the Sabine king Titus Tatius co-ruled with Romulus for several years until his death.

Romulus established many of Rome's early political and social institutions. He created the Senate, initially comprising 100 men chosen from the leading families. He also organized the army, creating the first legion of 3,000 infantry and 300 cavalry.

Despite these accomplishments, Romulus's rule became increasingly authoritarian over time. He was said to appear in public surrounded by 12 lictors carrying fasces, bundles of rods symbolizing his power to punish. This display of authority, along with other actions, created tension with the Senate.

After a 37-year reign, Romulus's rule came to a mysterious end. According to the most popular version of the story, recounted by Livy and Plutarch, Romulus disappeared in supernatural circumstances while reviewing his troops on the Campus Martius.

· · ·

Livy writes that during a sudden storm, Romulus was enveloped by a cloud. When the storm cleared, he had vanished. The senators present declared that Romulus had been taken up to heaven, becoming the god Quirinus. This narrative of apotheosis served to deify Romulus and reinforce Rome's divine origins.

However, both Livy and Plutarch mention an alternative, more sinister theory. Some believed the senators, tired of Romulus's autocratic rule, had murdered him during the storm, dismembered his body, and concealed the pieces. Each senator was said to have carried away a piece under his robe, disposing of it secretly.

The historian Dionysius of Halicarnassus provides additional context for the political tensions that might have led to Romulus's demise. He notes that Romulus had become increasingly tyrannical, adjudicating cases alone without counselors and appearing arrogant in his dress and manner.

To quell the unrest following Romulus's disappearance, a respected senator named Proculus Julius claimed that Romulus had appeared to him in a vision. According to

Proculus, Romulus declared that he had become a god and prophesied Rome's future greatness.

Whether through apotheosis or assassination, Romulus's reign ended, giving way to a period of interregnum before the next king, Numa Pompilius, took the throne. Numa was remembered as a peaceful counterpoint to the warrior-king Romulus, focusing on religious and legal reforms.

The story of Romulus, while largely mythical, reflects several historical realities of early Rome. The conflict with the Sabines likely represents the gradual synoecism (political unification) of separate settlements on Rome's hills. The abduction of the Sabine women might symbolize early marriage practices or political alliances.

Archaeological evidence supports some elements of the legend. Excavations on the Palatine Hill have revealed settlements dating back to the 8th century BCE, aligning with the traditional founding date of Rome. The discovery of an ancient stone wall, tentatively dated to the mid-8th century BCE, has been speculatively linked to the legendary walls of Romulus.

.   .   .

Regardless of its historical accuracy, the Romulus myth played a crucial role in Roman culture and identity. It provided a noble origin for the city, linking it to the god Mars. The tale of Romulus's apotheosis established a precedent for the later deification of emperors. The institutions supposedly created by Romulus - the Senate, the tribal system, the army - formed the backbone of the Roman state for centuries.

Even in the late Republic and Empire, Romans continued to honor Romulus. Julius Caesar claimed descent from him through the Julii family's connection to Aeneas. Augustus, Rome's first emperor, presented himself as a second Romulus, a new founder ushering in a golden age.

The story of Romulus endures as a founding myth that encapsulates themes of divine favor, fraternal strife, nation-building, and the tension between autocracy and shared governance. These themes resonated throughout Roman history and continue to captivate scholars and the public alike, ensuring that Romulus remains a central figure in our understanding of ancient Rome.

2

———

MUSSOLINI'S HIDDEN GOLD

In the waning days of World War II, as Allied forces pushed through Italy and Benito Mussolini's fascist regime crumbled, a legend was born. It spoke of a vast treasure, a hoard of gold hidden away by Il Duce himself. This tale of Mussolini's gold has captivated treasure hunters, historians, and conspiracy theorists for decades. But is there any truth to it, or is it just another wartime myth?

The story begins in 1943. Mussolini, once the unquestioned leader of Italy, found his power slipping away. The Allies had invaded Sicily, and the Italian people were turning against him. On July 25, the Grand Council of Fascism voted to limit his power, and King Victor Emmanuel III had him arrested. For a man who had ruled

Italy with an iron fist for over two decades, it was a stunning fall from grace.

But Mussolini's story wasn't over yet. In September, German paratroopers rescued him from his mountain prison, and Hitler installed him as the leader of a puppet state in northern Italy. It was during this period, from September 1943 to April 1945, that the legend of Mussolini's gold began to take shape.

According to various accounts, Mussolini, realizing that his days were numbered, began to make preparations for a post-war future. He allegedly ordered the collection of a vast amount of gold and other valuables. This treasure was said to include not only the personal wealth of Mussolini and other fascist leaders but also gold from the Italian central bank and even artifacts looted from Italy's rich cultural heritage.

The purpose of this gold hoard was twofold. First, it would provide Mussolini and his inner circle with the means to live comfortably in exile if they managed to escape. Second, and perhaps more importantly, it could fund a resurgence of the fascist movement in Italy after the war.

· · ·

But where did Mussolini hide this gold? This is where the story becomes murky, with multiple theories and alleged sightings over the years.

One of the most persistent theories places the gold in Rome itself. During his time in power, Mussolini had a network of bunkers and secret passages constructed beneath the city. These were ostensibly for protection against air raids, but they also provided perfect hiding places for secrets.

In 2011, Italian archaeologists made a surprising discovery beneath the Palazzo Venezia, Mussolini's former head-quarters. They uncovered a previously unknown bunker, a nine-room complex hidden beneath the 15th-century palazzo. This find sparked new interest in the legend of Mussolini's gold. If such a substantial bunker could remain hidden for over 60 years, what else might be concealed beneath Rome's streets?

Another theory focuses on Lake Como in northern Italy. In the final days of April 1945, as Allied forces closed in, Mussolini and his mistress, Clara Petacci, attempted to flee to Switzerland. They were part of a convoy that was stopped by Italian partisans near the village of Dongo on Lake Como.

According to some accounts, this convoy was carrying a substantial amount of gold and other valuables. Witnesses spoke of trucks loaded with heavy crates, guarded by German soldiers. But after Mussolini and Petacci were captured and executed, the gold seemingly vanished.

This has led to decades of speculation and treasure hunting around Lake Como. Some believe the gold was hidden in the mountains surrounding the lake. Others think it might have been sunk in the lake itself. Despite numerous searches, including efforts using advanced sonar equipment, no trace of the treasure has ever been found.

But the legend doesn't stop at Italy's borders. Some researchers believe that Mussolini's gold might have made its way out of the country entirely. One theory suggests that the treasure was smuggled into Switzerland, hidden among the vast amounts of Nazi gold that found its way into Swiss banks during the war.

. . .

Another, more outlandish theory claims that the gold was shipped to Argentina. In the post-war years, Argentina under Juan Perón became a haven for many former Nazi officials. Could Mussolini's gold have followed the same route? While there's no concrete evidence to support this idea, it has fueled imaginations and inspired works of fiction.

The story of Mussolini's gold isn't just about hidden treasure. It's also a tale of the chaotic final days of World War II in Italy, a time of shifting allegiances and desperate acts.

As the fascist regime collapsed, there were reports of widespread looting. Italian partisans, German soldiers, and even Allied troops were all accused of helping themselves to Italy's wealth. In this atmosphere of confusion and opportunism, it's entirely possible that any gold Mussolini had accumulated was simply stolen piecemeal, dispersed among numerous individuals rather than hidden as a single large cache.

. . .

This theory is supported by some historical records. In the days following Mussolini's capture and execution, Italian partisans recovered millions of lire in cash and valuables from fascist officials trying to flee the country. However, this was far less than what many believed Mussolini had accumulated.

The legend of Mussolini's gold has had a lasting impact on Italian culture and politics. In the immediate post-war years, accusations about the gold's whereabouts were often used as political weapons. Various groups accused each other of having stolen or hidden the treasure, using these claims to discredit their opponents.

The story has also inspired numerous books, documentaries, and even treasure hunting expeditions. In the 1960s, a group of former Italian partisans claimed to have a map showing where the gold was hidden in the mountains near Lake Como. Their expedition, while ultimately fruitless, attracted significant media attention and reignited interest in the legend.

More recently, in 2013, Italian police investigated claims that Mussolini's gold was hidden in a small town in Lombardy. A parish priest had reportedly confessed on his deathbed that he had helped hide the treasure in the 1940s. Despite extensive searches, including the use of metal detectors and ground-penetrating radar, no gold was found.

The enduring fascination with Mussolini's gold speaks to the power of wartime mysteries. World War II, with its global scale and countless untold stories, provides fertile ground for such legends. The idea of hidden Nazi gold has become a staple of popular culture, appearing in countless books and films. Mussolini's gold represents an Italian variant of this theme, tapping into the same mix of historical intrigue and treasure-hunting excitement.

But the legend also serves as a reminder of the dark legacy of Mussolini's regime. Any gold he might have hidden would have been accumulated through the exploitation of the Italian people and the plunder of occupied territories. The treasure, whether real or imaginary, represents the ill-gotten gains of a dictator who brought war and suffering to millions.

In recent years, historians have begun to approach the legend of Mussolini's gold more critically. While acknowledging that Mussolini and other fascist leaders likely did try to secure some wealth for themselves as their regime collapsed, many scholars doubt the existence of a vast, hidden treasure trove.

They point out that by 1945, Italy's economy was in shambles. Years of war had depleted the country's resources, and the fascist regime had already sold off much of Italy's gold reserves to fund its military campaigns. In this context, the idea that Mussolini could have amassed a huge quantity of gold seems unlikely.

Moreover, Mussolini's final days were marked by desperation and confusion, not careful planning. His attempt to flee to Switzerland was hastily organized and poorly executed. It seems improbable that he would have been able to coordinate the hiding of a vast treasure while simultaneously trying to save himself.

Despite these skeptical voices, the legend of Mussolini's gold persists. It continues to capture imaginations and inspire treasure hunters. Every few years, a new claim or discovery reignites interest in the story.

· · ·

In a way, the gold has taken on a life of its own, becoming part of Italy's cultural landscape. It represents not just a potential physical treasure, but also the unresolved questions and lingering shadows of the fascist era. As long as these questions remain, the legend of Mussolini's gold is likely to endure.

Whether the gold exists or not, the story serves as a powerful reminder of a turbulent period in Italian history. It speaks to the chaos of war's end, the desperation of a falling regime, and the human tendency to see mysteries and hidden treasures in the gaps of historical knowledge.

The tale of Mussolini's gold, with its mix of historical fact and imaginative speculation, continues to fascinate us. It's a story that connects the grand events of World War II with the timeless allure of hidden treasure. And as long as there are unsolved mysteries from that era, people will continue to wonder about the fate of Mussolini's gold.

3

___

THE STRANGE CASE OF THE GALLI

In ancient Roman religion, the Galli were priests dedicated to the worship of Cybele, the Phrygian goddess also known to Romans as Magna Mater or the Great Mother. Their practices, appearance, and role in Roman society provide insight into the integration of foreign religious traditions in the ancient world.

Cybele's cult originated in Phrygia, located in modern-day Turkey. She was a mother goddess associated with fertility, nature, and wild animals. Her consort was Attis, a youthful god whose myth was central to the cult's practices. The Romans encountered Cybele's worship during their expansion into the eastern Mediterranean and officially brought her cult to Rome in 204 BCE, during the Second Punic War against Carthage.

· · ·

The introduction of Cybele's worship to Rome was a strategic political and religious decision. The Roman Senate, seeking divine aid against Hannibal's forces, consulted the Sibylline Books. These prophetic texts advised bringing the "Idaean Mother" to Rome to ensure victory. The goddess was represented by a sacred black stone, likely a meteorite, which was transported from her shrine in Pessinus to Rome in an elaborate ceremony.

Initially, Cybele was worshipped at the Temple of Victory on the Palatine Hill. In 191 BCE, a temple dedicated specifically to her was built on the same hill. This central location indicated the importance accorded to her cult. The annual festival of Cybele, the Megalesia, became a significant event in the Roman calendar, celebrated from April 4th to April 10th.

The Galli, as Cybele's priests, were integral to her worship and became a distinctive presence in Roman religious life. Their name likely derived from the Gallus River in Phrygia, believed to inspire religious frenzy. The most notable aspect of the Galli was their practice of ritual self-castration, performed in imitation of Attis.

. . .

According to myth, Attis was a young shepherd beloved by Cybele. In one version of the story, he broke his vow of chastity to the goddess, then castrated himself in a fit of madness and died. Cybele's grief over his death was said to cause winter, while his rebirth brought spring. This cycle of death and rebirth was fundamental to the cult's beliefs and rituals.

The Galli's act of self-castration typically occurred during the Dies Sanguinis (Day of Blood) on March 24th, as part of the festival of Cybele and Attis. This festival, added to the Roman calendar in the 1st century CE, was a week-long event filled with intense emotions and dramatic rituals. It began with the carrying of reeds, symbolizing those that sheltered the infant Attis, followed by a period of fasting and lamentations. On the Dies Sanguinis, initiates into the priesthood would castrate themselves in a frenzied state, using a sharp implement. This act was seen as the ultimate devotion to the goddess, a complete renunciation of masculinity and earthly procreation in favor of a spiritual role.

After their castration, the Galli adopted an appearance and lifestyle that set them apart from traditional Roman society. They wore women's clothing, often brightly colored and elaborate. They grew their hair long and frequently bleached it blonde or white. They wore heavy makeup, jewelry, and often a tall, cylindrical hat called a mitra. This androgynous or feminine appearance was a visible sign of their special status and their rejection of traditional masculine roles.

The Galli's public appearances were characterized by ecstatic rituals that both fascinated and repelled Roman onlookers. During processions and festivals, they would dance through the streets to the rhythm of tympanons (hand drums), cymbals, and flutes. These dances often involved rapid, spinning movements. They would work themselves into a frenzy, flagellating themselves and even drawing blood as a devotional act.

The leader of the Galli was known as the Archigallus. Initially, Roman law forbade citizens from becoming Galli, reflecting a desire to maintain a distinction between Roman and foreign religious practices. The role of Archigallus was thus initially restricted to non-citizens, typically individuals of Phrygian origin. However, by the time of Emperor Claudius in the 1st century CE, this restriction was lifted, and Roman citizens could take on this role. The Archigallus wore distinctive regalia, including a gold crown with medallions depicting the gods of the cult.

Despite the official acceptance of Cybele's cult, the Galli themselves occupied an ambiguous and often marginalized position in Roman society. Their voluntary castration and adoption of feminine attributes conflicted with Roman ideals of masculinity and civic duty. Roman men were expected to be virile, procreate, and serve in the military - all roles that the Galli explicitly rejected.

This tension is reflected in Roman literature, where the Galli are often portrayed negatively. The poet Catullus, in his poem 63, depicts a young man who impulsively castrates himself to become a Gallus, only to immediately regret his irreversible decision. The satirist Juvenal mocks the Galli's appearance and behavior, portraying them as effeminate and morally suspect. Even Lucretius, in his philosophical work "De Rerum Natura," uses the Galli as an example of how religion can lead to extreme and irrational behavior.

However, it would be incorrect to assume that all Romans viewed the Galli with disdain. Their rituals, while shocking to many, held a powerful attraction for others. The ecstatic nature of their worship offered a stark contrast to the more restrained rituals of traditional Roman religion. For some, the Galli represented a form of divine madness, a direct and powerful connection to the divine that transcended normal social boundaries.

The Galli also played practical roles in Roman society beyond their religious duties. Many worked as fortune-tellers, a profession that was in high demand despite official disapproval. They were known to wander the streets with an image of Cybele, collecting alms and offering blessings or prophecies in return. Some may have worked in the sex trade, although the evidence for this is ambiguous and may reflect Roman prejudices more than historical reality.

The influence of the Galli and the cult of Cybele extended far beyond the city of Rome. As the Roman Empire expanded, so too did the worship of the Great Mother. Evidence of her cult has been found throughout the empire, from Britain to North Africa. In some cases, her worship merged with local mother goddess traditions, creating unique syncretic forms of religion.

In Britain, for example, altars dedicated to Cybele have been found along Hadrian's Wall, suggesting that her cult reached even the furthest corners of the empire. The remains of a sanctuary to Cybele in London include a ceremonial pine cone, a symbol associated with Attis, indicating that the full range of the cult's practices may have been performed there.

The cult of Cybele and the role of the Galli evolved over time. In the later Roman Empire, the philosophy of Neoplatonism influenced interpretations of the cult, with thinkers seeking to find deeper, allegorical meanings in its myths and rituals. The Emperor Julian, in his essay "On the Mother of the Gods," offered a complex philosophical interpretation of the myth of Attis, seeing in it a representation of the soul's descent into and liberation from the material world.

The fate of the Galli and Cybele's cult in the late Roman period is somewhat unclear. As Christianity gained dominance, traditional pagan cults came under increasing pressure. However, the cult of Cybele showed remarkable resilience. There is evidence that her worship continued in some form into the 4th century CE, with the last recorded celebration of the Megalesia taking place in 390 CE.

· · ·

Some scholars have suggested that certain aspects of Cybele's cult may have influenced early Christian practices and beliefs, particularly in relation to the Virgin Mary. The image of the mother goddess holding her divine son bears some resemblance to Christian iconography of Mary and Jesus. However, such comparisons are contentious and should be treated with caution.

The story of the Galli illustrates the religious diversity of the ancient Roman world. Their practices, alien to traditional Roman values, nonetheless found a place within the empire's religious landscape. The tension between acceptance and rejection of the Galli reflects broader Roman attitudes towards foreign cults - a mixture of fascination, revulsion, and pragmatic integration.

Moreover, the Galli challenge our modern categories of gender and sexuality. Their ritual castration and adoption of feminine attributes were not understood in terms of modern concepts of transgender identity, but rather as a unique religious status that transcended normal gender categories. This perspective offers a reminder of the cultural specificity of gender concepts and the diverse ways in which societies have conceived of gender roles.

. . .

The Galli remain somewhat enigmatic in historical records. Their voices do not come down to us directly, but rather through the often hostile or sensationalized accounts of Roman writers. Yet their enduring presence in Roman religion, lasting for centuries despite official ambivalence and popular scorn, testifies to the power of their religious message and the enduring human desire for ecstatic, transformative religious experiences.

The story of the Galli, with all its complexities and contradictions, continues to interest scholars and students of ancient religion. It offers a view into the diverse and sometimes shocking world of ancient Mediterranean religion, reminding us of the wide spectrum of human religious experience and the often surprising forms that devotion can take.

4

EMPEROR NERO'S GOLDEN HOUSE

In the heart of ancient Rome, a palace once stood that defied imagination. The Domus Aurea, or "Golden House," was Emperor Nero's grand vision - a sprawling complex that showcased the heights of Roman luxury and engineering. But its story is more than just one of opulence; it's a tale of ambition, controversy, and lasting influence that continues to captivate us today.

The year was 64 AD, and Rome was in chaos. A great fire had swept through the city, leaving much of it in ruins. As the smoke cleared and the citizens began to rebuild, Nero saw an opportunity. With vast swathes of the city now cleared, he could create something truly extraordinary - a palace that would outshine anything the world had ever seen.

· · ·

Nero enlisted the talents of two brilliant architects, Severus and Celer, to bring his vision to life. The result was a complex that stretched across 300 acres, encompassing parts of the Palatine, Oppian, and Esquiline hills. This wasn't just a single building, but a series of pavilions and structures set amidst lush gardens, vineyards, and even an artificial lake.

The scale of the Domus Aurea was staggering. Imagine walking through a palace so vast that it included its own countryside within the city walls. Visitors would have been awestruck by the sheer variety of landscapes - from manicured gardens to wild forests, from placid lakes to bubbling fountains. It wasn't just a home; it was an entire world crafted to Nero's specifications.

At the heart of this complex was the main palace, a marvel of Roman engineering and design. Its most famous feature was the coenatio rotunda, a rotating dining room that pushed the boundaries of what was thought possible in architecture. Picture yourself as a guest at one of Nero's lavish banquets. As you recline on your couch, the entire room begins to move, slowly revolving to mimic the movement of the celestial spheres. Above you, the domed ceiling opens, and a shower of flower petals and perfume rains down, filling the air with color and fragrance.

This wasn't just a gimmick, but a carefully orchestrated experience designed to overwhelm the senses. The rotating mechanism, hidden from view and operated by teams of slaves, was a feat of engineering that would be impressive even by today's standards. It speaks to the Roman ability to harness technology for the pursuit of pleasure and spectacle.

But the coenatio rotunda was just one of many wonders within the Domus Aurea. The Octagonal Room, another architectural marvel, featured a domed concrete ceiling with a central oculus - a design that predates and possibly influenced the famous Pantheon. Sunlight streaming through this opening would have created dramatic lighting effects, enhancing the room's already impressive decorations.

And what decorations they were! The interiors of the Domus Aurea were a testament to the skill of Roman artisans and the vast resources at Nero's disposal. Walls were covered in frescoes depicting mythological scenes, landscapes, and trompe l'oeil architectural elements that gave the illusion of even greater space. Precious stones and metals were used liberally - in fact, the name "Golden House" comes from the extensive use of gold leaf throughout the complex.

Mosaics of intricate design covered the floors, while statues imported from Greece and other parts of the empire added to the artistic wealth. The overall effect must have been dazzling, a sensory overload of color, texture, and craftsmanship.

One particularly noteworthy aspect of the Domus Aurea's design was its use of light. Roman architects were masters at manipulating natural light, and the palace showcased this skill brilliantly. Large windows, strategically placed openings, and reflective surfaces were used to illuminate the interior spaces, creating an ever-changing play of light and shadow throughout the day.

Water also played a crucial role in the palace's design. Beyond the artificial lake, which was large enough to simulate sea battles for entertainment, there were numerous fountains and water features throughout the complex. The sound of running water would have been a constant presence, adding to the sensory experience and helping to cool the air in Rome's hot summers.

But for all its beauty and innovation, the Domus Aurea was also deeply controversial. The fire that had cleared the way for its construction had devastated much of Rome, leaving many citizens homeless and destitute. Rumors quickly spread that Nero himself had started the fire to make room for his new palace. While modern historians doubt the truth of this claim, it speaks to the resentment many Romans felt towards their emperor's extravagant project.

The cost of the Domus Aurea, both in terms of resources and manpower, was enormous. At a time when much of Rome was struggling to rebuild, Nero's lavish spending on his personal residence seemed like a slap in the face to many citizens. The Roman historian Suetonius reported that Nero quipped, "At last I can begin to live like a human being," when he moved into the completed palace - a statement that, if true, would have only fueled public anger.

Despite the controversy, work on the Domus Aurea continued. Nero had grand plans for the complex, including a colossal statue of himself - the Colossus Neronis - that would stand over 100 feet tall. This statue, while impressive, would later be modified by subsequent emperors to represent the sun god Sol, erasing Nero's likeness but leaving a lasting mark on Rome's skyline.

Nero's reign, and with it the glory days of the Domus Aurea, came to an abrupt end in 68 AD. Faced with a military revolt and abandoned by his guards, Nero committed suicide. In the aftermath, Rome's new rulers had to decide what to do with the massive and controversial palace complex.

The reaction was swift and decisive. Nero's successors, eager to distance themselves from his legacy, set about dismantling or repurposing much of the Domus Aurea. The artificial lake was drained and filled in, becoming the site for the Flavian Amphitheater - better known today as the Colosseum. Other parts of the complex were buried and built over, effectively erasing much of Nero's grand vision from the Roman landscape.

The main palace itself was stripped of its valuables - its gold, precious stones, and many of its statues were removed and repurposed. The structure was then filled with earth up to the level of its vaulted ceilings, creating a strange buried world that would lie hidden for centuries.

This could have been the end of the Domus Aurea's story, a cautionary tale about the excesses of imperial power. But fate had other plans. In the late 15th century, a young Roman fell through a crack in the ground on the Oppian Hill and found himself in a strange cave filled with painted figures. Word of this discovery spread quickly among Rome's artists, and soon many were lowering themselves into these "grottoes" to study the ancient paintings.

Among these artists were some of the greatest names of the Renaissance, including Raphael and Michelangelo. They were amazed by the freshness and vibrancy of the 1500-year-old frescoes, preserved by their burial. The style of these paintings, with their delicate, fantastical designs, would go on to influence Renaissance art significantly. In fact, the term "grotesque" in art derives from these rediscovered "grottoes" of the Domus Aurea.

This rediscovery sparked a renewed interest in the Domus Aurea and its creator. Excavations began, slowly revealing more of the palace's secrets. However, these early excavations were often haphazard and caused significant damage to the already fragile structures.

Today, the remains of the Domus Aurea continue to be a source of fascination for archaeologists and historians. Ongoing excavation and restoration work is slowly piecing together more of Nero's vision. Visitors can now tour parts of the complex, walking through rooms that once hosted the elite of Roman society.

Modern technology is also helping to bring the Domus Aurea back to life. Virtual reality reconstructions allow visitors to see the palace as it might have looked in its prime, with its vibrant colors and intricate decorations restored. These digital recreations offer a glimpse into the truly awe-inspiring nature of Nero's creation.

The story of the Domus Aurea is more than just a tale of ancient luxury. It's a testament to the ambition and skill of Roman architects and artists, pushing the boundaries of what was possible in their time. It's a cautionary tale about the dangers of imperial excess and the fickle nature of legacy. And it's a reminder of the enduring power of art and architecture to inspire and influence across the centuries.

. . .

As we continue to uncover and understand more about the Domus Aurea, we gain not just knowledge about a single building, but insights into the society that created it. In its soaring ambitions and controversial history, in its fall and rediscovery, the Golden House offers us a unique window into the complexities of Roman imperial power and the lasting impact of one emperor's grand vision.

5

THE ENIGMA OF THE PONS SUBLICIUS

In the early days of Rome, when the city was still finding its footing as a power in the Italian peninsula, a simple wooden bridge changed the course of history. The Pons Sublicius, believed to be the oldest bridge in Rome, was more than just a way to cross the Tiber River. It was a marvel of engineering, a stage for heroic deeds, and a focal point for religious rituals that would shape Roman culture for centuries to come.

The story of the Pons Sublicius begins around 642 BCE, during the reign of Ancus Marcius, the legendary fourth king of Rome. Ancus Marcius, known for his expansion of Roman territory and his efforts to strengthen the city's defenses, recognized the need for a bridge across the

Tiber. This wasn't just about convenience; it was a strategic move that would connect the heart of Rome to the Janiculum Hill on the western bank, a critical defensive position.

But building a bridge across the swift-flowing Tiber was no small feat. The Romans faced a dilemma: they needed a bridge strong enough to withstand the river's currents and heavy traffic, but also one that could be quickly dismantled in case of an enemy attack. The solution they came up with was ingenious.

The Pons Sublicius was constructed entirely of wood, without a single metal nail or bolt. Instead, the wooden beams were joined using an intricate system of joints and pegs. This design allowed the bridge to be quickly taken apart if enemies approached from the west, denying them easy access to the city. The name "Sublicius" itself comes from the Latin word for "wooden beams" or "piles," reflecting its unique construction.

This innovative design was a testament to Roman engineering prowess. Building a sturdy bridge without metal fasteners required precise craftsmanship and a deep understanding of structural mechanics. The bridge had to withstand not only the daily traffic of people and goods but also the Tiber's frequent floods. Its success paved the way for future Roman bridge-building projects, setting a standard for ingenuity and practicality that would become hallmarks of Roman engineering.

The Pons Sublicius quickly became an integral part of Roman life. It connected the Forum Boarium, Rome's cattle market and commercial hub, with the western bank of the Tiber. This linkage spurred economic growth and helped integrate the areas west of the river more closely with the city proper. But it wasn't long before the bridge would prove its worth in a more dramatic fashion.

In 508 BCE, Rome faced one of its greatest early challenges. The city had recently overthrown its last king, Tarquinius Superbus, and established itself as a republic. But Tarquinius wasn't going to give up his throne without a fight. He enlisted the help of Lars Porsena, the powerful king of Clusium, to lead an Etruscan army against Rome.

As the Etruscan forces approached the city, the Romans found themselves in a desperate situation. The enemy was at the gates, and the city's defenses were not yet strong enough to withstand a prolonged siege. It was at this moment that the Pons Sublicius, and a Roman hero named Horatius Cocles, would enter the annals of legend.

Horatius, along with two companions, Spurius Larcius and Titus Herminius, took up position at the western end of the bridge. Their mission was simple but seemingly impossible: hold off the entire Etruscan army long enough for their fellow Romans to destroy the bridge behind them, denying the enemy access to the city.

As the Etruscans charged, Horatius and his companions stood firm. They fought with a ferocity that gave pause even to the battle-hardened Etruscans. One by one, Etruscan warriors fell before their swords. But the odds were overwhelming, and soon Horatius ordered his companions back across the bridge while he continued to fight alone.

The scene, as described by ancient historians, was one of incredible bravery. Horatius, a single figure silhouetted against the setting sun, facing down an entire army. Behind him, the sounds of Roman axes chopping at the wooden beams of the bridge filled the air. The Etruscans, both awed and enraged by Horatius's stand, peppered him with missiles, but still he fought on.

. . .

Finally, with the bridge creaking and groaning behind him, Horatius heard the shouts of his fellow Romans telling him it was done. The bridge was nearly destroyed. It was at this moment that Horatius did something that would be retold for generations. Still fully armed, he leaped into the Tiber.

The river god Tiberinus, so the story goes, was so impressed by Horatius's bravery that he bore him safely to the eastern shore. Horatius emerged from the river to the cheers of his fellow Romans, having saved the city through his incredible act of self-sacrifice.

This tale of Horatius at the bridge became one of Rome's most cherished legends. It embodied the Roman virtues of courage, selflessness, and devotion to the state. Horatius was honored with a statue in the comitium, the public meeting place in Rome, and his deed was celebrated in song and story for centuries. Even today, the phrase "Horatius at the bridge" is used to describe someone making a heroic last stand against overwhelming odds.

. . .

But the Pons Sublicius was more than just a backdrop for heroic deeds. It also played a crucial role in Roman religious life. One of the most enigmatic rituals associated with the bridge was the ceremony of the Argei.

Each year on May 15th, the Vestal Virgins, accompanied by Rome's highest religious and civic officials, would proceed to the Pons Sublicius. There, they would throw straw effigies, called Argei, into the Tiber. The exact meaning of this ritual has been lost to time, but theories abound.

Some scholars believe it was a substitute for human sacrifice, a way for the Romans to appease the river god without actually taking human life. Others see it as a symbolic cleansing of the city, with the effigies representing the sins or impurities of the past year being washed away by the Tiber's waters. Whatever its original meaning, the ritual of the Argei continued for centuries, underscoring the Pons Sublicius's importance as a liminal space, a bridge not just between physical places but between the mundane and divine realms.

The religious significance of the Pons Sublicius extended beyond this annual ritual. The care and maintenance of the bridge were entrusted to a special college of priests called the Pontifices. In fact, the word "Pontifex," which later came to mean "bridge-builder" and was applied to the high priest of Rome (and later to the Pope), may have originally referred specifically to the priests responsible for the Pons Sublicius. This connection between bridge-building and religious authority highlights the deep spiritual significance the Romans attached to this seemingly mundane piece of infrastructure.

As Rome grew and changed over the centuries, so too did the Pons Sublicius. The original wooden structure was rebuilt multiple times, sometimes after being destroyed by floods or warfare. In later years, it was reconstructed in stone, losing its original function as a quickly-dismantled defense but gaining in durability. Yet even as the physical bridge changed, its place in Roman culture and imagination remained strong.

The area around the Pons Sublicius became steeped in legend and superstition. Stories circulated of strange sights and sounds near the bridge, especially at night or during storms. Some claimed to have seen ghostly figures reenacting Horatius's famous stand, while others reported hearing the clash of spectral swords on windswept nights. Whether these tales were born of genuine experiences or were simply the product of the bridge's storied history, they added to its mystique.

One persistent legend told of people disappearing while crossing the bridge, especially on foggy nights. These disappearances were sometimes attributed to the river god Tiberinus, claiming unwary travelers as sacrifices. Other stories spoke of treasure hidden beneath or near the bridge, guarded by supernatural forces. While likely no more than folklore, these tales speak to the powerful hold the Pons Sublicius had on the Roman imagination.

As Rome entered its imperial phase, the Pons Sublicius gradually lost its practical importance. Newer, larger bridges were built across the Tiber, better suited to the needs of a growing metropolis. Yet the old bridge continued to be maintained, more for its historical and religious significance than for any practical purpose.

The last recorded repair of the Pons Sublicius took place in the 5th century CE, during the twilight years of the Western Roman Empire. After this, the bridge fades from historical records. Whether it was finally destroyed by a flood, deliberately dismantled, or simply allowed to decay is unknown. Today, no trace of the original Pons Sublicius remains visible.

Yet the legacy of Rome's first bridge lives on. The site where it once stood, near the modern Ponte Sublicio, remains a place of historical interest. Archaeologists continue to search the area and the riverbed for any remnants of the ancient structure. More importantly, the stories associated with the Pons Sublicius – Horatius's brave stand, the ritual of the Argei, the legends of ghostly sightings – continue to captivate those interested in Roman history and mythology.

The Pons Sublicius serves as a powerful reminder of the ingenuity, bravery, and spiritual depth of ancient Rome. It shows us how a simple structure – a wooden bridge across a river – can become imbued with layers of meaning, becoming a symbol of a city's identity and values. From its practical origins as a defensive measure to its role in religious rituals and its place in heroic legend, the Pons Sublicius embodies the complex interweaving of the practical and the symbolic that characterized so much of Roman culture.

. . .

In the end, the story of the Pons Sublicius is more than just the tale of a bridge. It's a window into the soul of ancient Rome, a testament to the power of engineering, bravery, and belief to shape not just a physical landscape, but the cultural and spiritual landscape of a civilization. Though the bridge itself has long since vanished beneath the waters of the Tiber, its legacy continues to inspire and intrigue us, bridging the vast gulf of time between ancient Rome and the present day.

6

THE VATICAN NECROPOLIS

Beneath the grandeur of St. Peter's Basilica, below the ornate marble floors and soaring domes, lies a world frozen in time. This is the Vatican Necropolis, an ancient city of the dead that has slumbered in darkness for nearly two millennia. Its discovery in the 20th century sent shockwaves through the archaeological and religious communities, offering tantalizing clues about the early Christian church and potentially the final resting place of St. Peter himself.

The story of the necropolis begins long before the basilica that now stands above it. In the 1st century AD, the area was on the outskirts of ancient Rome, a slope of the Vatican Hill that served as a burial ground. It was here, according to Christian tradition, that St. Peter was martyred and buried around 64 AD during the persecutions of Emperor Nero.

For centuries, the exact location of Peter's tomb was lost to history. The original modest memorial was replaced by increasingly grand structures as Christianity grew from a persecuted sect to the official religion of the Roman Empire. By the 4th century, the Emperor Constantine had built a basilica over what was believed to be Peter's burial site. This church stood for over a thousand years before being replaced by the current St. Peter's Basilica in the 16th century.

All the while, the ancient necropolis lay buried and forgotten beneath layers of history and construction. It wasn't until the 20th century that its existence would come to light, thanks to a combination of historical detective work and sheer chance.

The rediscovery began in 1939 when plans were underway to build a tomb for Pope Pius XI in the Vatican Grottoes, the level beneath the main floor of St. Peter's. As workers excavated, they stumbled upon something unexpected: ancient Roman mausoleums, perfectly preserved and adorned with frescoes, mosaics, and inscriptions.

. . .

This chance discovery sparked a decade-long archaeological excavation that would uncover a vast necropolis dating back to the 1st century AD. The dig was carried out in utmost secrecy, with only a handful of people aware of what lay beneath one of Christianity's holiest sites.

What the archaeologists found was astonishing. The necropolis was a veritable street of the dead, with row upon row of mausoleums lining a sloping path. These tombs belonged to both pagans and early Christians, offering a unique glimpse into the religious diversity of ancient Rome.

The pagan mausoleums were elaborate affairs, decorated with colorful frescoes depicting scenes from classical mythology. Inscriptions spoke of the lives and deeds of the deceased, while niches held urns containing their ashes. These tombs told the story of a Roman upper class that still clung to traditional beliefs even as Christianity was beginning to take hold.

. . .

Interspersed among these pagan tombs were simpler Christian burials. These graves were marked with symbols like the chi-rho, an early representation of Christ's name, and contained bodies rather than ashes, reflecting the Christian belief in bodily resurrection.

As the excavations continued, the archaeologists' excitement grew. They were getting closer to the area directly beneath the high altar of St. Peter's, the traditional site of the apostle's burial. In 1942, they made a discovery that would electrify the Christian world: a set of bones wrapped in purple cloth shot through with gold thread, contained in a niche behind a wall covered with ancient graffiti.

One piece of graffiti, in particular, caught their attention. It read "Petros eni," which translates to "Peter is here." Could this be the long-lost tomb of St. Peter?

The Vatican was cautious in its claims, but the possibility was tantalizing. Further investigation revealed that the bones belonged to a robust man in his 60s or 70s, consistent with what was known about Peter at the time of his death. The purple and gold cloth suggested a burial of great importance.

. . .

However, the story of Peter's tomb is not without controversy. Some scholars have questioned the dating of the bones and the interpretation of the graffiti. The complex history of the site, with multiple phases of construction and renovation over the centuries, makes definitive conclusions difficult.

Regardless of whether the bones truly belong to St. Peter, the necropolis itself is a treasure trove of historical and archaeological information. It offers a unique window into the world of 1st and 2nd century Rome, a time when Christianity was still a small, often persecuted sect struggling to establish itself in the heart of the pagan empire.

The tombs tell stories of families and individuals long forgotten by history. There's the mausoleum of the Valerii, with its beautiful stucco decorations and portrait busts of the deceased. The tomb of Flavius Agricola bears a poignant inscription urging passersby to enjoy life while they can. These personal touches humanize the ancient Romans, reminding us that they, too, loved, mourned, and sought to be remembered.

. . .

The necropolis also provides valuable information about early Christian burial practices and beliefs. The gradual shift from cremation to inhumation, the use of Christian symbols alongside traditional Roman iconography, and the development of martyr cults can all be traced through the changing styles of tombs and inscriptions.

Perhaps most importantly, the necropolis offers tangible evidence of the early Christian community in Rome. The fact that Christians were buried alongside pagans suggests a degree of social integration that challenges some traditional narratives about the early church. The presence of both humble and elaborate Christian tombs indicates a diverse community that included both poor and wealthy members.

Today, the Vatican Necropolis is open to a limited number of visitors each day. Those lucky enough to secure a spot on a tour descend into a world that feels frozen in time. The air is cool and damp, heavy with the weight of centuries. As you walk along the ancient street, you're treading the same path as mourners and pilgrims from nearly two thousand years ago.

. . .

The tour culminates at the place believed to be Peter's tomb, now incorporated into a complex shrine that spans multiple levels of history. Here, separated by mere feet from the bustling basilica above, visitors can contemplate the foundations of the Catholic Church in a very literal sense.

The discovery and excavation of the Vatican Necropolis have had far-reaching implications beyond archaeology and history. For many Christians, particularly Catholics, the potential identification of St. Peter's tomb provides a powerful physical connection to the origins of their faith. It's a reminder that the grand basilica above is built not just on stone foundations, but on the lives and deaths of generations of believers.

For scholars, the necropolis offers a wealth of data about life, death, and belief in ancient Rome. The intermingling of pagan and Christian burials provides insight into the gradual Christianization of the empire. The artistic styles and funerary practices documented in the tombs help fill gaps in our understanding of Roman social and cultural history.

.   .   .

The necropolis has also sparked ongoing debates about the relationship between archaeology and faith. How do we balance scientific inquiry with religious tradition? What role should physical evidence play in matters of belief? These questions continue to resonate as archaeologists and theologians grapple with the implications of discoveries beneath St. Peter's.

As you emerge from the cool darkness of the necropolis into the soaring spaces of the basilica above, the contrast is striking. From the intimate, personal memorials of the dead, you rise into a space designed to inspire awe and emphasize the grandeur of the church. Yet both spaces serve the same fundamental human needs: to remember, to believe, to connect with something greater than ourselves.

The Vatican Necropolis reminds us that beneath the monumental architecture and centuries of tradition, Christianity began as a small community of believers, gathering in secret to remember their dead and celebrate their faith. It's a powerful testament to how much can change over two thousand years, and how much remains the same.

.   .   .

In the end, whether or not the bones in that ancient niche truly belong to St. Peter may be less important than what the necropolis as a whole represents. It's a direct link to the world in which Christianity was born, a physical reminder of the real people who lived, died, and believed at a pivotal moment in history. As long as it endures beneath the great basilica, the Vatican Necropolis will continue to inspire wonder, spark debate, and connect us to our shared past.

7

THE CATACOMBS AND MARTYRS OF ANCIENT ROME

eneath the bustling streets of Rome, a hidden city stretches for miles. This labyrinth of tunnels and chambers, carved into the soft tufa rock, tells a story of faith, persecution, and endurance. These are the catacombs of Rome, the underground cemeteries that once housed the dead and sheltered the living during the early days of Christianity.

The catacombs began as simple burial grounds in the 2nd century AD. Roman law forbade burial within the city walls, so communities began to inter their dead in the soft volcanic rock outside the city. For the early Christians, a persecuted minority in pagan Rome, these underground necropolises became more than just cemeteries. They were sanctuaries, places of worship, and eventually, the stuff of legend.

As you descend into the catacombs, the noise of the modern city fades away. The air grows cool and damp, heavy with the weight of centuries. Narrow passageways branch off in all directions, their walls lined with loculi - rectangular niches carved to house the dead. In the flickering light of candles or electric lamps, faded frescoes emerge from the darkness, depicting scenes from scripture or symbols of early Christian faith.

The early Christians didn't invent the catacombs, but they embraced them with a fervor that transformed these burial grounds into sacred spaces. As the Christian community grew, so did the catacombs. Layer upon layer was excavated, creating a vast underground network that stretched for hundreds of kilometers.

But it wasn't just the dead who occupied these subterranean chambers. During times of persecution, when being a Christian could mean a death sentence, the living sought refuge in the catacombs. Hidden from the prying eyes of Roman authorities, they would gather to worship, to break bread, and to strengthen their faith.

. . .

It's from this period of secrecy and danger that many of the legends of the catacombs emerge. Tales of brave martyrs, miraculous escapes, and divine intervention echo through these underground halls. One of the most famous is the story of Saint Cecilia, a young noblewoman said to have been martyred in the 3rd century.

According to legend, Cecilia was sentenced to death for her Christian faith. The Roman prefect ordered her to be locked in the caldarium, or steam room, of her own house and suffocated. But when the executioners opened the room after a day and a night, they found Cecilia alive and unharmed, the steam having had no effect on her. Enraged, the prefect ordered her beheaded. The executioner struck her neck three times, but failed to sever her head. Cecilia lingered for three days, preaching and praying, before finally succumbing to her wounds.

Cecilia's body was said to have been buried in the Catacomb of Callixtus, one of the largest and most important of Rome's underground cemeteries. Today, visitors can see a statue in the catacombs depicting Cecilia in the position her body was allegedly found centuries later -

lying on her side, her fingers outstretched in a final profession of faith.

Another compelling legend is that of Saints Nereus and Achilleus, two Roman soldiers who converted to Christianity and were martyred for their faith. Their bodies were buried in what is now known as the Catacomb of Domitilla. According to tradition, the two saints appeared centuries after their death to workers excavating the catacombs, directing them to the location of their tomb.

These stories of martyrdom and miraculous intervention became a crucial part of early Christian identity. The catacombs, with their hidden chambers and secret symbols, provided the perfect backdrop for tales of faith triumphing over persecution. Whether these stories were literal truth or spiritual allegory, they served to inspire and unite the Christian community.

As Christianity spread and eventually became the official religion of the Roman Empire, the catacombs gradually fell out of use as burial sites. By the 5th century, most burials were taking place in churches or aboveground cemeteries. The catacombs were still visited as pilgrimage sites, but over time, many were forgotten or lost.

. . .

It wasn't until the 16th century that the catacombs began to recapture the imagination of Rome. In 1578, workers accidentally discovered an entrance to one of the lost catacombs. This rediscovery sparked a renewed interest in early Christian history and archaeology. Scholars and adventurers began to explore the underground networks, uncovering ancient artifacts and deciphering centuries-old inscriptions.

One of the most significant figures in catacomb exploration was Antonio Bosio, often called the "Columbus of the Catacombs." Bosio spent decades exploring and mapping the underground cemeteries, publishing his findings in a groundbreaking work, "Roma Sotterranea" (Underground Rome). His work laid the foundation for the scientific study of the catacombs, a field that continues to yield new discoveries to this day.

As exploration of the catacombs continued, new legends began to emerge. Stories circulated of explorers getting lost in the maze-like tunnels, never to be seen again. Some claimed to have encountered the ghosts of ancient Christians, still guarding their underground sanctuaries. Others spoke of hidden chambers filled with priceless relics or secret passages leading to unknown parts of the city.

These modern myths added a new layer to the catacombs' mystique. They became a popular subject for gothic novels and horror stories, their dark, winding passages serving as the perfect setting for tales of terror and the supernatural. Even today, the catacombs continue to inspire writers, filmmakers, and artists, their ancient mysteries translated into new forms for new audiences.

But beyond the legends and ghost stories, the catacombs remain a place of profound historical and spiritual significance. They offer a unique window into the lives and deaths of ancient Romans, both pagan and Christian. The inscriptions and artwork found in the catacombs provide invaluable information about early Christian beliefs and practices, as well as the social and cultural dynamics of ancient Rome.

For many modern visitors, descending into the catacombs is a powerful experience. The silence, the darkness, the tangible sense of history - all combine to create a atmosphere that's both eerie and awe-inspiring. Standing in chambers where people gathered to worship two thousand years ago, or seeing the final resting places of individuals who lived and died in ancient Rome, creates a connection to the past that's hard to find anywhere else.

As archaeological techniques have advanced, our understanding of the catacombs has deepened. New technologies like ground-penetrating radar and 3D mapping have revealed previously unknown chambers and passages. Chemical analysis of bones and artifacts has provided new insights into the lives and deaths of those buried in the catacombs. Each new discovery adds another piece to the puzzle of Rome's underground history.

Yet for all our scientific knowledge, the catacombs retain an air of mystery. In the dim light and close confines of these ancient tunnels, it's easy to imagine the whispered prayers of hunted Christians, the quiet defiance of those who chose faith over safety. The legends of martyrs and miracles, whether historically accurate or not, speak to the human capacity for belief and sacrifice.

Today, several of Rome's catacombs are open to the public, offering guided tours that blend historical fact with traditional legends. Visitors can walk the same paths trod by ancient Romans, see the tombs of early Christians, and marvel at frescoes that have survived for nearly two millennia. It's a journey not just through physical space, but through time itself.

As you emerge from the catacombs back into the sunlight and noise of modern Rome, the contrast is striking. The city above has been built and rebuilt countless times since the days when Christians first began to bury their dead in these underground chambers. But beneath the streets, the catacombs remain largely as they were, a preserved slice of ancient life and death.

The story of Rome's catacombs and the legends of its early Christian martyrs is more than just a historical curiosity. It's a testament to the enduring power of faith, the human need for community in the face of adversity, and the ways in which the past continues to shape our present. In the winding tunnels beneath Rome, the whispers of centuries past still echo, inviting us to listen and remember.

8

THE GHOST OF VIA VENETO

Rome's Via Veneto stretches like a ribbon of glamour through the heart of the Eternal City. Its sidewalks have felt the tread of movie stars, its cafes have hosted whispered conversations between politicians and artists, and its hotels have sheltered the secrets of the rich and famous. But among the glitz and the glamour, there's a darker tale that's whispered in the quiet hours of the night - the story of the ghost that haunts one of Via Veneto's grand hotels.

The street first rose to international fame in the 1950s and 60s, during the era known as "La Dolce Vita" - the sweet life. Federico Fellini's 1960 film of the same name captured the essence of this time, portraying a Rome filled with hedonistic pleasures and moral decay. Via Veneto was at the heart of it all, a playground for the beautiful and the damned.

It was during this time that the legend of the ghost began to take shape. The story goes that a young woman - some say an actress, others a socialite - met her end in one of the street's luxurious hotels. The details of her demise are as varied as the people who tell the tale. Some say she was murdered, perhaps by a jealous lover or a rival for her affections. Others claim it was a tragic accident - a fall from a balcony after one too many glasses of champagne, or a slip on a marble staircase.

Whatever the cause, her death left more than just a body behind. It left a restless spirit, one that has been seen wandering the halls of the hotel for decades.

The first reported sighting came from a maid in the early 1960s. She was cleaning a room when she felt a sudden chill. Turning around, she saw a woman standing by the window, gazing out at the street below. The woman was dressed in an elegant gown that seemed to shimmer in the afternoon light. But when the maid blinked, the figure was gone.

. . .

Since then, the sightings have continued. Guests have reported seeing a beautiful young woman in the mirrors of their rooms, only to turn around and find no one there. Others have felt an unseen presence watching them as they sleep, or heard the rustle of silk in empty corridors.

One particularly vivid account comes from an American tourist who stayed at the hotel in the 1980s. He woke in the middle of the night to find a woman sitting at the foot of his bed. She was weeping silently, her shoulders shaking with each sob. The tourist, more curious than afraid, asked her what was wrong. The woman turned to him, revealing a face of haunting beauty marked by infinite sadness. She opened her mouth as if to speak, but no words came out. Instead, she simply faded away, leaving the tourist with a feeling of profound loss.

The hotel staff, for their part, have learned to live with their spectral resident. Some even see her as a kind of mascot, a link to the hotel's glamorous past. They've given her a name - Giulia - though no one knows if this was actually her name in life.

. . .

One long-time bellhop, who's worked at the hotel for over 40 years, claims to have seen Giulia multiple times. "She's not scary," he insists. "Just sad. Like she's looking for something she can't find."

But who was this woman in life? And what keeps her tied to the hotel after death? These are questions that have tantalized ghost hunters and historians alike for years.

One theory suggests that she was a rising starlet in the Italian film industry. Rome in the 1950s was a hotbed of cinematic activity, with American productions like "Roman Holiday" and "Cleopatra" bringing Hollywood glamour to the city's ancient streets. Perhaps our ghost was an actress on the cusp of stardom, her life cut short before she could see her name in lights.

Another theory paints a darker picture. In the world of "La Dolce Vita," not everything was as sweet as it seemed on the surface. Behind the parties and the paparazzi flashes, there were often power struggles and dangerous liaisons. Could our ghost have been a pawn in some larger game, her death the result of knowing too much about the wrong people?

．　．　．

There are even those who believe that the ghost is not one woman, but many - a composite of all the broken dreams and shattered hopes that Via Veneto has witnessed over the years. In this interpretation, she's less a specific individual and more a symbol of the dark side of the dolce vita lifestyle.

Whatever the truth, the ghost of Via Veneto has become an integral part of Rome's modern mythology. She's a reminder that even in a city as ancient as Rome, new legends are still being born.

The ghost's fame has spread beyond the confines of the hotel. Today, she's a staple of Rome's ghost tours, which take visitors on a journey through the city's spookier side. These tours often start on Via Veneto as the sun is setting, when the street takes on a different character. The bright cafes and boutiques give way to deepening shadows, and the bustling crowds thin out. It's in this twilight atmosphere that the ghost stories seem most plausible.

Tour guides regale their groups with tales of Giulia's appearances, embellishing the story with each retelling.

They point out the hotel where she supposedly died, its windows dark and mysterious in the gathering dusk. Some swear they can sometimes see a figure in one of the upper windows, watching the street below.

But the ghost of Via Veneto is just one of many supernatural tales that haunt Rome's streets. The city's long and often violent history has given rise to countless ghost stories. There's the headless spirit that's said to wander near the Castel Sant'Angelo, believed to be the ghost of Beatrice Cenci, executed for the murder of her abusive father. Or the phantom monk who appears in the Colosseum at night, possibly a victim of the gladiatorial games held there centuries ago.

These stories reflect Rome's complex relationship with its past. In a city where ancient ruins stand alongside modern buildings, where every shovelful of earth might uncover some long-buried artifact, the line between past and present often seems blurry. Is it any wonder, then, that the dead sometimes seem to linger?

The ghost of Via Veneto, however, holds a special place in this pantheon of spirits. Unlike many of Rome's other ghosts, she's a relatively recent addition to the city's supernatural landscape. She represents not the weight of ancient history, but the allure and danger of Rome's more recent past.

Her story resonates with many because it taps into the mythos of "La Dolce Vita" era. This was a time when Rome was at the center of the world's attention, when it seemed like anything was possible. But it was also a time of excess and moral ambiguity, when the pursuit of pleasure could lead to dire consequences. The ghost of Via Veneto embodies both the glamour and the danger of this era.

Over the years, the ghost has inspired more than just tours and tales. She's been the subject of poems, short stories, and even a low-budget Italian horror film in the 1970s. In these retellings, her story often takes on new dimensions. Sometimes she's portrayed as a tragic victim, other times as a femme fatale who got her just deserts. In some versions, she's even given a measure of redemption, finally finding peace after decades of haunting.

But for all the stories and speculation, the true identity of the ghost - if she ever existed at all - remains a mystery. The hotel staff are tight-lipped about any actual deaths that may have occurred on the premises, citing privacy concerns. Historical records from the time are incomplete, and the fast-paced, celebrity-filled world of 1950s Rome left behind more gossip than hard facts.

This lack of concrete information has only added to the ghost's mystique. In the absence of facts, imagination has free rein. Each person who hears the story can fill in the blanks for themselves, creating their own version of who this woman might have been and what might have led to her untimely end.

Today, Via Veneto is still a place of luxury and excitement, though perhaps not quite as wild as in its heyday. The cafes still buzz with conversation, the hotels still host the rich and famous, and the high-end shops still display goods most can only dream of affording. But now there's an added attraction - the thrill of possibly encountering a ghost from the street's glamorous past.

For skeptics, the ghost of Via Veneto is nothing more than a clever marketing ploy, a way to add a frisson of excitement to an already popular tourist destination. They point out that ghost sightings tend to increase during the peak tourist season, and that many of the most dramatic encounters conveniently happen to people who are already familiar with the legend.

But for believers, no amount of skepticism can shake their faith in the ghost's existence. They point to the consistency of the sightings over the years, the emotional impact reported by witnesses, and the simple fact that in a city as old and storied as Rome, anything is possible.

Whether you believe in ghosts or not, the legend of Via Veneto's spectral resident adds another layer to Rome's already rich history. It's a reminder that every place has its stories, its secrets, its unresolved mysteries. In a city that's seen emperors and popes, saints and sinners, artists and criminals, why not a ghost or two as well?

As night falls on Via Veneto and the street lamps cast their warm glow, it's easy to imagine that glamorous, troubled era of decades past. And if you look closely at the windows of that grand old hotel, who knows? You might just catch a glimpse of a beautiful woman in an elegant gown, still searching for whatever it is that keeps her bound to this world. Just remember - in Rome, the past is never really past. It lives on in the stones of the buildings, in the stories passed down through generations, and sometimes, just sometimes, in the restless spirits that refuse to say goodbye.

9

———

THE MIRACLE OF ST. PETER'S CHAINS

In the heart of Rome, not far from the Colosseum, stands a church that holds a secret. San Pietro in Vincoli, or Saint Peter in Chains, isn't the largest or most famous of Rome's churches, but it guards a treasure that has drawn pilgrims for centuries: the chains that once bound Saint Peter, the rock upon which the Christian church was built.

But in 1950, this ancient church became the scene of an event that would add a new chapter to its long history. It was the year of the great Jubilee, when Rome was flooded with pilgrims from around the world. Among them was a nun, whose name has been lost to time, but whose experience would be remembered for generations.

.   .   .

The story goes that on a quiet afternoon, as the nun knelt in prayer before the altar where St. Peter's chains are kept, something extraordinary happened. The chains, encased in their reliquary for safekeeping, began to move. They lifted and shifted, as if animated by an unseen force. The nun, at first disbelieving her own eyes, watched in awe as the ancient links clinked and rustled, defying the laws of nature.

When the movement ceased, the nun, shaken but filled with a sense of wonder, reported what she had seen to the church authorities. News of the event spread quickly, first among the clergy, then to the faithful in Rome, and eventually to Catholics around the world. Many saw it as a divine sign, a miracle that reaffirmed the sanctity of the chains and the power of faith.

But to understand the full significance of this event, we need to step back and look at the history of San Pietro in Vincoli and the chains it houses.

The story begins in the 5th century, with a woman named Licinia Eudoxia. She was the daughter of one Roman emperor, the wife of another, and a woman of great influence. According to tradition, Eudoxia's mother had given her a set of chains, said to be those that had bound St. Peter when he was imprisoned in Jerusalem.

Eudoxia decided that these holy relics deserved a fitting home. She commissioned the construction of a basilica on the Esquiline Hill in Rome, specifically to house the chains. The church was completed around 439 AD, and from the beginning, it was closely associated with the chains it protected.

But there was more to the story. Rome already had a set of chains said to have bound St. Peter, these from his imprisonment in the Mamertine Prison in Rome before his execution. When Pope Leo I was presented with Eudoxia's chains from Jerusalem, he decided to compare them with the Roman chains.

What happened next became one of the foundational legends of San Pietro in Vincoli. As Pope Leo held the two sets of chains close to each other, they miraculously fused together, forming a single, unbroken chain. This event was seen as a divine confirmation of the chains' authenticity and a symbol of the unity of the Church.

· · ·

From that moment on, San Pietro in Vincoli became an important pilgrimage site. The chains were displayed in a special reliquary under the main altar, visible to the faithful who came to venerate them. Pilgrims believed that praying before the chains could lead to healing, forgiveness, and spiritual renewal.

Over the centuries, San Pietro in Vincoli saw its share of changes and additions. In the 15th century, it became the titular church of Cardinal Giuliano della Rovere, who would later become Pope Julius II. It was Julius who commissioned Michelangelo to create a grand tomb for him, to be placed in the basilica.

Michelangelo's plans for the tomb were ambitious - perhaps too ambitious. What was meant to be a massive, free-standing monument with forty statues was eventually scaled down to a wall tomb. But from this project came one of Michelangelo's most famous works: the statue of Moses.

The Moses dominates the lower part of Julius's tomb, which was finally completed long after both the pope and Michelangelo had died. The powerful figure of the biblical prophet, with his piercing gaze and flowing beard, has become almost as much of an attraction as the chains themselves.

The basilica also houses other artistic treasures. There are frescoes by Jacopo Coppi depicting the miracle of the chains. The ceiling of the sacristy is decorated with a fresco by Giovanni Battista Parodi, showing St. Peter being freed from prison by an angel. In the apse, a painting by Guercino depicts the death of St. Margaret.

But despite all this artistic splendor, it's the chains that have always been the heart of San Pietro in Vincoli. They've survived sackings, fires, and the tumultuous history of Rome itself. They've been a constant presence, a tangible link to the early days of Christianity and to St. Peter himself.

Which brings us back to that afternoon in 1950, when a nun saw those ancient chains move.

The event caused a sensation. Skeptics dismissed it as a trick of the light, or perhaps a small earthquake that went unnoticed by others. Some suggested that the nun, caught up in the fervor of the Jubilee year, had simply imagined the whole thing.

But for many, the moving chains were a powerful sign. They saw it as a message from St. Peter himself, a reminder of the enduring power of faith. Some even connected it to the dogma of the Assumption of Mary, which Pope Pius XII would proclaim later that same year.

The church authorities investigated the event, interviewing the nun and others who were in the basilica at the time. While they never officially declared it a miracle, they didn't dismiss it either. The story was allowed to spread, becoming part of the oral tradition of San Pietro in Vincoli.

In the years since, the tale of the moving chains has become intertwined with the longer history of the basilica. Guides tell it to visitors, often in hushed tones as they stand before the reliquary. It's become another layer in the rich history of this place, a modern miracle in an ancient church.

· · ·

But beyond the question of whether the chains really moved that day, the story speaks to something deeper about San Pietro in Vincoli and places like it. These ancient churches, with their relics and artwork, are more than just monuments to the past. They're living spaces where history, faith, and the possibility of the miraculous intersect.

Every day, people from all over the world visit San Pietro in Vincoli. Some come for the art, eager to see Michelangelo's Moses up close. Others come as tourists, checking another site off their list of Rome's must-see attractions. And still others come as pilgrims, drawn by the chains and what they represent.

For these pilgrims, the chains are a physical link to the beginnings of their faith. They touch the glass of the reliquary, perhaps imagining the touch of St. Peter himself. They pray, hoping that somehow, across the centuries, their words will reach the saint who once wore these bonds.

And sometimes, if you watch closely, you might see someone glance quickly at the chains, then look again more intently. Perhaps they're remembering the story of the nun and her miraculous vision. Perhaps they're hoping, just for a moment, that they too might witness something extraordinary.

In the end, whether you believe in miracles or not, there's something undeniably powerful about San Pietro in Vincoli. It's a place where the past feels very close, where ancient stories come to life, and where, just maybe, the impossible can happen.

As you leave the cool, quiet interior of the basilica and step back out into the Roman sunshine, you might find yourself looking at the city a little differently. In a place like Rome, where every stone seems to have a story, San Pietro in Vincoli reminds us that new chapters are still being written. The miracle of the moving chains is just one of them – who knows what the next might be?

10

THE GHOSTLY CHOIR OF THE PANTHEON

In the heart of Rome stands a building that has defied time. The Pantheon, with its perfect dome and oculus open to the sky, has watched over the Eternal City for nearly two thousand years. But as the sun sets and tourists drift away, some say the Pantheon harbors a secret - a ghostly choir whose ethereal voices echo through its vast chamber.

The story begins, as many Roman tales do, in the twilight between day and night. A time when the last rays of sunlight slip away from the Pantheon's marble floors, and the great bronze doors close with a resonant thud. It's then, in the quiet hours, that the mysterious music begins.

.   .   .

Visitors lingering in the piazza outside have reported hearing faint strains of choral music drifting from within the closed building. The voices, they say, are unlike any earthly choir. They seem to come from everywhere and nowhere at once, filling the night air with haunting melodies that speak of ages past.

Many Romans who live near the Pantheon insist they've heard the ghostly music multiple times. It's always late at night, when the square is empty. The music is described as beautiful but sad, like a lament for something lost long ago.

But what could be the source of this phantom choir? To unravel this mystery, we need to delve into the Pantheon's long and complex history.

The building we see today isn't the original Pantheon. The first was built around 27 BC by Marcus Agrippa, right-hand man to Emperor Augustus. That structure, however, was destroyed by fire. The Pantheon we know was rebuilt by Emperor Hadrian around 126 AD, though he modestly retained Agrippa's original inscription on the facade: "M. AGRIPPA L.F. COS. TERTIUM FECIT" (Marcus Agrippa, son of Lucius, built this during his third consulship).

. . .

Hadrian's Pantheon was a marvel of Roman engineering and design. Its massive dome, 142 feet in diameter, was the largest in the world for centuries. At its apex is the oculus, a 30-foot wide opening that allows sunlight (and sometimes rain) to pour into the interior. This perfect circle of sky gives the Pantheon an otherworldly quality, a sense of connection between earth and heavens that must have been awe-inspiring to ancient worshippers.

For the Romans, the Pantheon was a temple to all the gods - that's what its name means in Greek. But in 609 AD, the building was converted into a Christian church, consecrated to St. Mary and the Martyrs. This transformation saved the Pantheon from the fate that befell many other Roman structures, which were stripped of their marble and bronze to be used in newer buildings.

It's this long history of worship, both pagan and Christian, that some believe gives rise to the ghostly choir. Could the phantom voices be the echoes of ancient Roman priests, still chanting their devotions to Jupiter, Mars, and Venus? Or perhaps they're the spirits of early Christian martyrs, singing praises to their God in the face of persecution?

· · ·

Others point to the Pantheon's notable burials as a possible source of the spectral music. The tombs of several Italian kings are housed here, as well as that of the great Renaissance artist Raphael. Some speculate that the ghostly choir might be connected to these illustrious dead, a kind of eternal requiem for the great figures of the past.

But not everyone believes the choir is supernatural in origin. Skeptics argue that the Pantheon's unique acoustics might be playing tricks on people's ears. The building's perfect proportions and domed ceiling create an unusual sound environment. Even today, a whisper uttered on one side of the rotunda can be clearly heard on the opposite side.

Acoustic engineers who've studied the Pantheon offer a possible explanation. The building acts like a giant whispering gallery. Sounds from outside - even distant sounds - can be focused and amplified by the dome. What people might be hearing is actually a choir practicing in one of Rome's many nearby churches, distorted and etherealized by the Pantheon's acoustics.

· · ·

This scientific explanation, however, doesn't account for all the reports. Many witnesses insist they've heard the choir when the area around the Pantheon was completely silent. And then there's the nature of the music itself - described as unlike anything heard in modern churches.

Musicologists specializing in ancient Roman music find the descriptions intriguing. The witnesses often describe the music as 'otherworldly' or 'ancient-sounding'. This could be suggestive of the kind of music that might have been performed in the Pantheon during Roman times - very different from the Christian liturgical music we're familiar with today.

The legend of the Pantheon's ghostly choir has become a part of Rome's modern folklore. Ghost tours of the city often stop outside the building, regaling tourists with tales of the phantom singers. Some brave (or foolhardy) souls have even attempted to spend the night in the piazza, hoping to capture the elusive music on recording devices. So far, no one has managed to produce convincing evidence of the choir's existence - but that hasn't stopped people from trying.

·   ·   ·

The story has also inspired artists and writers. Several novels have been written featuring the Pantheon's choir as a plot element, and more than one composer has created pieces inspired by the legend. In recent years, immersive art installations in the piazza have used hidden speakers to recreate the effect of the ghostly choir, giving visitors a taste of what the experience might be like.

But beyond the ghost stories and legends, the tale of the Pantheon's choir speaks to something deeper about our relationship with history and the built environment. The Pantheon has stood for nearly two millennia, a silent witness to the ebb and flow of empires, the rise and fall of beliefs. It's seen Rome transform from the capital of a vast empire to a medieval backwater, and then rise again as the heart of the Catholic world and a modern European capital.

In the face of such vast stretches of time, it's natural for us to imagine echoes of the past lingering in ancient stones. The idea of a ghostly choir in the Pantheon touches on our desire to connect with history, to hear the voices of those long gone. It's a reminder that the past is never truly dead - it lives on in the structures we inherit and the stories we tell about them.

. . .

Moreover, the legend of the choir underscores the Pantheon's enduring mystery. Despite being one of the most studied buildings in the world, the Pantheon still holds secrets. How did the Romans create its perfect dome without modern technology? What was the exact purpose of the oculus? These questions, like the source of the ghostly music, continue to puzzle experts and fascinate the public.

As night falls over Rome and the Pantheon stands silhouetted against the darkening sky, it's easy to understand why people might hear ghostly music in the air. The building itself seems to demand something more than mundane explanation. Its perfect proportions, its dome seemingly suspended without support, the oculus open to the heavens - all of these elements combine to create a sense of the numinous, a feeling that here, perhaps, the veil between worlds grows thin.

Whether you believe in ghosts or not, the next time you find yourself in Rome, it might be worth lingering in the Piazza della Rotonda as night falls. Stand in the shadow of the Pantheon's great columns, close your eyes, and listen. Perhaps you'll hear the splash of water from Bernini's fountain, or the chatter of late-night revelers in a nearby cafe. Or perhaps, if you're very lucky (or unlucky, depending on your perspective), you might catch the faint strains of an ancient melody, drifting on the night air - the voices of Rome's long history, still singing after all these years.

In the end, the story of the Pantheon's ghostly choir is more than just a spooky tale. It's a testament to the power of great architecture to inspire our imaginations, to connect us with the past, and to make us ponder the mysteries of existence. As long as the Pantheon stands - and it has already stood for longer than many nations have existed - people will continue to visit it, to wonder at it, and to listen for the echoes of history in its ancient stones.

11

THE ETRUSCAN PYRAMIDS OF BOMARZO

T ime has a way of hiding even the grandest of human achievements. For centuries, a monumental structure lay hidden in plain sight, its weathered steps slowly disappearing beneath a blanket of vegetation. This wasn't some minor relic, but a pyramid - not in Egypt or Mexico, but in the rolling hills of Lazio, a stone's throw from Rome itself.

The Etruscan Pyramid of Bomarzo stands as a testament to a civilization that flourished long before Rome cast its shadow across the Mediterranean. Unlike its more famous cousins along the Nile, this pyramid doesn't reach for the sky with smooth limestone blocks. Instead, it's carved from a single massive piece of volcanic rock, a feat of engineering that would be impressive even by today's standards.

Rising about 16 meters from the forest floor, with potentially another 7 or 8 meters hidden underground, the Bomarzo pyramid is a monument to Etruscan ingenuity. A series of precisely cut steps leads to a flat platform at the top, hinting at its possible use as an altar or observation point. But for all its grandeur, this marvel of ancient architecture remained largely forgotten until the dawn of the 21st century.

Local folklore had long spoken of a strange stepped rock in the woods, but few outsiders paid attention to these tales. It wasn't until a curious local, armed with determination and a machete, decided to investigate. Hacking away years of overgrowth, he revealed the full extent of the monument, sending shockwaves through the archaeological community.

Here was tangible proof of the Etruscans' architectural prowess, a monumental work that rivaled those of other great ancient civilizations. But it also raised a host of questions. Who exactly built it? What was its purpose? And how had such a significant structure remained hidden for so long?

To understand the Bomarzo pyramid, we need to delve into the world of the Etruscans. This sophisticated civilization dominated central Italy from about 800 BC to 264 BC, before being absorbed into the expanding Roman Republic. The Etruscans were renowned for their art, their engineering skills, and their complex religious practices. They built great cities, developed a unique language, and traded extensively throughout the Mediterranean.

Yet for all their achievements, much about the Etruscans remains shrouded in mystery. They left few written records, and much of what we know comes from their elaborate tombs and the often-biased accounts of Greek and Roman writers. The Bomarzo pyramid adds another piece to this complex puzzle, offering a rare glimpse into Etruscan monumentality.

One of the most striking features of the pyramid is the precision of its carving. The steps are cut with remarkable evenness, the angles sharp and true, the surfaces smooth to the touch. This level of craftsmanship would be impressive even with modern tools. That the Etruscans achieved it over two millennia ago, using bronze chisels and iron hammers, speaks volumes about their capabilities and dedication.

Equally intriguing are the channels carved into the pyramid's surface. These grooves snake down the sides, converging at certain points. Their purpose has sparked heated debate among researchers. Some believe they were designed for the drainage of liquids, possibly blood from sacrificial rituals. This theory aligns with what we know of Etruscan religious practices, which often involved animal sacrifice to appease their pantheon of gods.

However, this interpretation isn't universally accepted. The steps leading to the top show surprisingly little wear, which seems odd if the pyramid had been used regularly for ceremonies over many years. This inconsistency has led to alternative theories about its function.

Some researchers propose that the pyramid may have been a temple for more peaceful rituals. In this view, the channels might have been used for ceremonial washing, with purifying water rather than sacrificial blood flowing down the sides. Others suggest that the structure was primarily symbolic, perhaps representing the Etruscan view of the cosmos or serving as a monumental tomb for a revered leader.

The pyramid's location adds another layer of intrigue to its purpose. From its top platform, one can see for miles across the Lazio countryside. This commanding view has led some to speculate that the pyramid may have had astronomical significance. The Etruscans, like many ancient peoples, were keen observers of the sky. They might have used this vantage point to track the movements of celestial bodies, timing their religious observances to the rhythms of the heavens.

But the Bomarzo pyramid doesn't stand in isolation. The surrounding area is dotted with other curious structures: smaller stepped platforms, cube-shaped stones with carved cavities, and other rock-cut features. These findings suggest that the pyramid was part of a larger sacred landscape, the full extent of which we're only beginning to understand.

The discovery of the Bomarzo pyramid has also ignited discussions about potential connections between the Etruscans and other ancient cultures. The stepped pyramid design bears a striking resemblance to structures found in Mesoamerica, while the concept of a sacred high place is common to many ancient religions. While most scholars are skeptical of direct links between these far-flung civilizations, the similarities are nonetheless intriguing.

As news of the pyramid spread, it began to draw visitors from far and wide. History enthusiasts and curious tourists alike come to see this enigmatic structure for themselves, to climb its ancient steps and ponder its mysteries. Standing at its base, looking up at the carved rock rising towards the sky, it's easy to feel a connection to the people who created it thousands of years ago.

For the town of Bomarzo, the pyramid has become a source of pride and a boost to the local economy. The town was already known for its 16th-century "Park of Monsters," a garden filled with grotesque sculptures. Now it has another unique attraction to offer visitors, one that speaks to a much older and more mysterious past.

Efforts are underway to further study and preserve the Bomarzo pyramid. Archaeologists hope that careful excavation might reveal more about the structure's original extent and purpose. There's also interest in using modern technology, such as ground-penetrating radar, to investigate what might lie beneath the pyramid without disturbing the site.

The pyramid's emergence has also rekindled interest in other potential Etruscan sites in the area. Both professional archaeologists and enthusiastic amateurs are scouring the countryside, looking for other forgotten monuments. Their efforts have already yielded results, with several other potentially significant sites identified in recent years.

As research continues, the Bomarzo pyramid serves as a reminder of how much we still have to learn about the ancient world. It challenges our perceptions of pre-Roman Italy, showing us a landscape that was more complex and diverse than we often imagine. The Etruscans were capable of monumental works that rivaled those of their more famous contemporaries in Greece and Egypt.

The pyramid also speaks to the enduring human fascination with the unknown. In a world where we often feel that everything has been discovered and explained, it offers a glimpse of mystery, a puzzle from the past that we're still trying to solve. Each year brings new theories, new discoveries, and new questions.

But perhaps the most powerful aspect of the Bomarzo pyramid is how it connects us to our distant ancestors. As we study this remarkable structure, we're not just learning about the Etruscans – we're gaining insight into the human drive to create, to build monuments that outlast their creators, to reach for the sky.

The pyramid reminds us that the urge to leave a mark on the world, to create something that will endure long after we're gone, is a fundamental part of human nature. The Etruscans who carved this monument couldn't have imagined that people would still be marveling at their work thousands of years later. Yet here we are, still climbing their steps, still pondering their mysteries.

Whether the Bomarzo pyramid was a place of sacrifice, a celestial observatory, or something else entirely, it stands as a testament to the ingenuity and ambition of an ancient people. It invites us to look at the landscape around us with new eyes, to wonder what other marvels might be hiding in plain sight, waiting for their moment to emerge from the passage of time.

As daylight fades and the first stars appear above the pyramid's weathered peak, it's easy to imagine the Etruscans who once gathered here. Perhaps they came to offer sacrifices to their gods, to chart the movements of the planets, or simply to marvel at the work of their own hands. Whatever their purpose, they left behind a monument that continues to inspire wonder and spark imagination more than two millennia later.

The story of the Bomarzo pyramid is far from over. Each new discovery, each new theory, adds another chapter to this ongoing tale. And as we continue to unravel its mysteries, we're not just learning about a single structure or a single civilization. We're gaining a deeper understanding of our shared human heritage, our age-old quest to understand our place in the universe, and our enduring desire to leave something of ourselves for future generations to ponder.

The Etruscan Pyramid of Bomarzo stands not just as a relic of the past, but as a bridge between ancient wisdom and modern curiosity. It challenges us to think beyond our preconceptions, to consider the capabilities of civilizations long gone, and to remain open to the wonders that still await discovery. In its weathered stone and enigmatic channels, we find not just the legacy of the Etruscans, but a reflection of our own enduring quest for knowledge and meaning.

12

THE DISAPPEARANCE OF ETTORE MAJORANA

Genius often walks a fine line between brilliance and obscurity. In the case of Ettore Majorana, that line blurred into one of the 20th century's most perplexing mysteries. A prodigy in theoretical physics, Majorana's mind grappled with the fundamental nature of reality, only to vanish as enigmatically as the quantum particles he studied.

Born in Sicily in 1906, Majorana's intellect shone early. By his mid-twenties, he had already made groundbreaking contributions to nuclear and particle physics. His peers, including Nobel laureate Enrico Fermi, spoke of him with a mixture of awe and frustration. Majorana could solve complex problems in his head, often arriving at solutions so quickly that others struggled to follow his reasoning.

.   .   .

Majorana's crowning achievement was the equation that bears his name. The Majorana equation predicted the existence of particles that are their own antiparticles, a concept that continues to fascinate physicists today. This work, along with his other contributions, placed him at the forefront of the quantum revolution that was reshaping our understanding of the universe.

As part of the "Via Panisperna boys," a group of young scientists led by Fermi, Majorana was at the epicenter of physics research in Rome. This team, named after the street where their laboratory was located, would go on to make crucial discoveries in nuclear physics. Yet, even among these brilliant minds, Majorana stood out for his unique insights and mathematical prowess.

But brilliance often comes at a price. Majorana was known for his reclusiveness and periods of intense work followed by withdrawal. Colleagues described him as shy and often melancholic. As the 1930s progressed, these traits seemed to intensify. He became increasingly isolated, even from his closest collaborators.

.   .   .

Then, in March 1938, the unthinkable happened. Majorana boarded a boat from Palermo to Naples and simply vanished. The circumstances surrounding his disappearance were as puzzling as they were sudden. Just before leaving, he had withdrawn all his money from the bank. He left behind a series of letters that hinted at a momentous decision but gave no clear indication of his intentions.

One letter to his family spoke of an "unavoidable necessity," while another to a colleague mentioned a decision that was "perfectly coherent with the nature of my theory." These cryptic messages only deepened the mystery. Was Majorana planning suicide? Had he chosen to disappear voluntarily? Or was there a more sinister explanation?

The timing of Majorana's disappearance added another layer of intrigue. Europe was on the brink of war, and the race for nuclear technology was intensifying. Majorana's expertise in nuclear physics made him a potential asset in this high-stakes competition. Some speculated that he might have been kidnapped by a foreign power eager to exploit his knowledge.

. . .

Others proposed more fantastical theories. Could Majorana have discovered something so profound, so potentially dangerous, that he felt compelled to remove himself from the world? The nature of his work, dealing with the fundamental building blocks of the universe, lent itself to such speculation.

As news of Majorana's disappearance spread, the Italian authorities launched an extensive search. Fermi himself appealed to Mussolini to intensify the efforts to find his brilliant colleague. But despite these efforts, no trace of Majorana was found. It was as if he had simply ceased to exist, like one of the quantum particles he studied winking out of reality.

Over the decades, various sightings and theories have emerged. Some claimed to have seen Majorana in Argentina, living under an assumed name. A photograph from the 1950s, showing a man bearing a striking resemblance to the missing physicist, fueled these speculations. Others insisted he had retreated to a monastery, seeking solace in spirituality rather than science.

The possibility of suicide remained a persistent theory. The waters between Palermo and Naples were searched, but no body was ever found. Friends and family pointed to Majorana's withdrawn nature and the hints of finality in his farewell letters as evidence for this explanation. Yet, the lack of concrete evidence left room for doubt.

As the years passed, Majorana's disappearance took on an almost mythical quality. It became a story not just about a missing scientist, but about the nature of genius itself. What drives someone to push the boundaries of human knowledge? And at what cost?

Majorana's legacy lived on in the world of physics. His prediction of particles that are their own antiparticles, known as Majorana fermions, continued to intrigue researchers. Decades after his disappearance, scientists began searching for these elusive particles in earnest. Their potential applications in quantum computing added a modern urgency to Majorana's theoretical work.

The mystery also captured the imagination of writers and artists. Novels, plays, and films explored various scenarios of what might have happened to the brilliant physicist. In these stories, Majorana became a symbol of the enigmatic nature of scientific discovery, of the thin line between genius and madness.

· · ·

In 2011, the case took an unexpected turn. The Rome Attorney's Office officially reopened the investigation into Majorana's disappearance. Using modern forensic techniques, they analyzed the photograph from Argentina and other pieces of evidence. While their findings were inconclusive, they did suggest that Majorana might have survived well past 1938.

This renewed interest sparked fresh debate about the ethical implications of Majorana's potential choices. If he had indeed chosen to disappear, leaving behind his work and the potential for its misuse, was this an act of cowardice or one of profound moral courage? In an age where scientific discoveries can have world-altering consequences, Majorana's story raised questions about the responsibilities of those at the cutting edge of knowledge.

The disappearance of Ettore Majorana remains unsolved, a puzzle that continues to intrigue and perplex. It's a story that touches on some of the most fundamental questions of science and human nature. What drives us to explore the unknown? How do we balance the pursuit of knowledge with its potential consequences? And what happens when the weight of that knowledge becomes too much to bear?

In the end, perhaps the most fitting tribute to Majorana is the ongoing relevance of his work. Every time a physicist searches for Majorana fermions or applies his equations, they are, in a sense, continuing the work of the brilliant mind that vanished so mysteriously. Majorana may have disappeared, but the ripples of his genius continue to spread through the scientific world.

The enigma of Ettore Majorana serves as a reminder of the human element in scientific discovery. Behind every equation and theory is a person grappling not just with the mysteries of the universe, but with their own place within it. In Majorana's story, we see the price of brilliance, the allure of the unknown, and the enduring power of an unsolved mystery.

As we continue to push the boundaries of scientific knowledge, the tale of the vanishing genius remains relevant. It challenges us to consider not just what we can discover, but how those discoveries shape us. In the end,

Majorana's greatest legacy may not be the equations he left behind, but the questions his disappearance continues to pose – about science, about humanity, and about the nature of reality itself.

13

THE CORPSE ON TRIAL

The year was 897, and Rome was about to witness one of the most bizarre and gruesome spectacles in its long history. The stage was set not in the Colosseum, where countless bloody spectacles had unfolded, but in the hallowed halls of the Basilica of St. John Lateran. The accused was not some living criminal, but a corpse - the body of Pope Formosus, dead for months and now exhumed to face judgment.

This was the Cadaver Synod, a macabre trial that would shock even a city accustomed to violence and intrigue. At its center stood Pope Stephen VI, a man consumed by hatred for his predecessor and determined to destroy Formosus's legacy, even if it meant putting a rotting corpse on trial.

. . .

To understand how such a ghastly event could occur, we must delve into the chaotic world of 9th century Rome. The papacy, far from being the stable institution we know today, was a hotbed of political intrigue and violence. Popes were not just spiritual leaders but powerful political figures, and the throne of St. Peter was a prize fought over by rival factions of Roman nobility.

Formosus had been a controversial figure long before his death. Born around 816, he had risen through the church ranks to become Bishop of Porto. His ambition and political maneuvering had made him enemies, and in 876, he was excommunicated by Pope John VIII on charges of conspiring against the pope and coveting the papal throne.

Formosus fled Rome, swearing an oath never to return or reclaim his former position. But oaths, it seemed, meant little in the cutthroat world of papal politics. By 883, Formosus was back in Rome, restored to his position by the new Pope Marinus I. Eight years later, in 891, Formosus achieved his long-held ambition and was elected pope himself.

. . .

His papacy was marked by political turmoil. He crowned two different Holy Roman Emperors, first Guido of Spoleto and then Lambert of Spoleto, before turning against them and inviting Arnulf of Carinthia to invade Italy. These shifting alliances made him many enemies among the Italian nobility.

Formosus died in April 896, and was succeeded by Boniface VI, who himself lasted only 15 days before dying. Then came Stephen VI, a man with a deep-seated hatred for Formosus and a willingness to go to extraordinary lengths to discredit him.

In January 897, Stephen VI ordered that Formosus's body be exhumed and brought to the Lateran for trial. The corpse, now nine months dead, was dressed in papal vestments and propped up on a throne to face its accusers. A deacon was appointed to answer on behalf of the deceased pontiff.

The charges against Formosus were numerous: that he had perjured himself, that he had coveted the papacy, that he had violated church law by serving as Bishop of Rome while already Bishop of Porto. Each charge was read out to the moldering corpse as if it could defend itself.

Witnesses were called, evidence was presented, and all the while, the stench of decay filled the air. The assembled clerics and nobles must have watched in a mixture of horror and morbid fascination as this grotesque farce played out before them.

To no one's surprise, the verdict was guilty. Stephen VI, acting as both prosecutor and judge, pronounced his sentence. Formosus was declared to have been unworthy of the papacy. All his acts and ordinations as pope were annulled. The three fingers of his right hand used for blessings were hacked off.

But even this was not enough to satisfy Stephen's hatred. He ordered that Formosus's papal vestments be torn from the corpse. The body was then dressed in common clothes and buried in a pauper's grave. But even this indignity was not the end. Shortly after, the corpse was exhumed once again and thrown into the Tiber River.

· · ·

The Cadaver Synod shocked even the hardened sensibilities of 9th century Rome. It was seen by many as an act of desecration, a violation of the sanctity of death and the papacy itself. The people of Rome, already suffering from famine and political instability, began to turn against Stephen VI.

Within months of the synod, a popular uprising broke out. Stephen was seized, stripped of his papal vestments, and thrown into prison. There, he was strangled to death - a grim echo of the indignities he had inflicted on Formosus's corpse.

The aftermath of the Cadaver Synod was as chaotic as the event itself. The next pope, Romanus, lasted only four months before being deposed. His successor, Theodore II, held the papacy for a mere twenty days. During his brief reign, Theodore worked to rehabilitate Formosus's memory, retrieving his body from the Tiber and giving it a proper burial in St. Peter's Basilica.

The controversy over Formosus's papacy and the legitimacy of his acts continued to rage. In 898, Pope John IX held another synod which declared the Cadaver Synod invalid and ordered all records of it destroyed. But the debate was far from over. In 904, Pope Sergius III, who had participated in the original trial as a co-judge, reversed John IX's decision and reaffirmed the findings of the Cadaver Synod.

The Cadaver Synod stands as one of the most bizarre episodes in papal history. It's a stark reminder of how far the papacy had fallen from its spiritual ideals, becoming a pawn in the power struggles of Roman nobility. The willingness to desecrate a papal corpse for political gain speaks volumes about the moral bankruptcy of the institution at that time.

But the story of the Cadaver Synod is more than just a historical curiosity. It raises profound questions about the nature of justice, the limits of power, and the respect due to the dead. Even in death, it seems, one is not safe from the machinations of the living.

The event also highlights the complex relationship between politics and religion in medieval Europe. The papacy was not just a spiritual office but a political one, with real temporal power. Popes commanded armies, made and broke alliances, and wielded significant influence over the affairs of kingdoms and empires. In this context, the Cadaver Synod can be seen as an extreme example of political theater, a way for Stephen VI to delegitimize his predecessor and consolidate his own power.

The Cadaver Synod had lasting repercussions for the Catholic Church. It contributed to a period known as the "Saeculum obscurum" or "Dark Age" of the papacy, a time of moral and spiritual decline that would not end until the reforms of the 11th century. The spectacle of a dead pope on trial undermined the dignity and authority of the papal office, weakening the church's position at a time when it faced significant challenges from secular rulers.

In the centuries since, the Catholic Church has worked hard to distance itself from the excesses of this period. The Cadaver Synod is rarely mentioned in official histories, an embarrassing episode best forgotten. Yet it remains a source of fascination for historians and the public alike, a vivid reminder of a time when the papacy was capable of acts that seem almost unthinkable today.

The story of the Cadaver Synod has inspired numerous works of art and literature over the years. It's been the subject of poems, plays, and novels, each trying to capture the macabre absurdity of the event. In these retellings, the trial often serves as a metaphor for the corruption of power and the dangers of unchecked authority.

Perhaps the most enduring legacy of the Cadaver Synod is the questions it continues to raise. How do we judge the actions of the dead? Can a corpse be held accountable for the deeds done in life? What are the limits of ecclesiastical and political power? These are questions that resonate beyond the specific context of 9th century Rome, touching on fundamental issues of justice, morality, and human nature.

As we look back on the Cadaver Synod from the vantage point of the 21st century, it's easy to dismiss it as a relic of a more barbaric age. But perhaps we should be cautious about such judgments. While we may no longer put corpses on trial, the human impulses that drove Stephen VI - hatred, ambition, the desire for vengeance - are still very much with us.

The next time you visit St. Peter's Basilica in Rome, take a moment to think about Formosus. Somewhere beneath the magnificent Renaissance architecture, his bones lie at rest, finally at peace after their posthumous ordeal. His story serves as a reminder of the dark chapters in the church's history, the depths to which human beings can sink, and the strange twists that history can take.

The Cadaver Synod may have been a singular event, but its themes - the abuse of power, the manipulation of justice, the desecration of the sacred - are sadly universal. In studying this grim episode from the past, perhaps we can gain insights that will help us navigate the moral and ethical challenges of our own time.

As the sun sets over Rome and the shadows lengthen across St. Peter's Square, one might almost imagine the ghost of Formosus wandering the Vatican grounds. Does his spirit still seek justice? Or has he forgiven those who so grotesquely violated his eternal rest? The Cadaver Synod remains a chilling reminder that even in death, we are not always allowed to rest in peace.

14

THE MYSTERIOUS DEATH OF POPE JOHN PAUL I

Smoke rose from the Sistine Chapel on August 26, 1978, signaling to the world that a new pope had been chosen. The man who emerged onto the balcony of St. Peter's Basilica was Albino Luciani, now Pope John Paul I. With a warm smile that would earn him the nickname "The Smiling Pope," he greeted the faithful gathered below. None could have imagined that just 33 days later, that smile would be forever stilled, leaving behind one of the most enduring mysteries in Vatican history.

John Paul I's papacy was notable for its brevity and the promise of change it seemed to herald. He eschewed the papal coronation, opting instead for a simpler inauguration. He spoke of reform, of a church more attuned to the needs of the poor. His humility and warmth endeared him to many, both within the Church and beyond.

But on the morning of September 29, 1978, the world woke to shocking news. Pope John Paul I was dead. Found in his bed, still wearing his glasses and with papers scattered around him, the 65-year-old pontiff had seemingly passed away in the night. The official cause: a heart attack.

Yet almost immediately, questions began to swirl. Why had the Vatican initially claimed that a papal secretary had discovered the body, when it was later revealed to have been Sister Vincenza Taffarel, a nun who had served John Paul I for years? Why was there no autopsy, despite the unexpected nature of the death? And why did the Vatican seem so eager to embalm the body and prepare for a new conclave?

These questions formed the foundation of what would become a decades-long cottage industry of conspiracy theories and speculation. At the heart of many of these theories was the idea that John Paul I had been murdered, silenced before he could enact sweeping reforms that would have threatened powerful interests within the Church.

. . .

One of the most prominent theories suggested that the pope was on the verge of exposing corruption within the Vatican Bank. This narrative painted a picture of a pontiff determined to clean house, targeting not just financial improprieties but also the influence of Freemasonry within the Church. According to this theory, John Paul I had been poisoned to prevent him from revealing these secrets.

Other theories focused on the pope's rumored plans to change Church doctrine on contraception or to remove conservative elements from positions of power. Some even suggested involvement from outside forces, from the KGB to the Italian Mafia.

Adding fuel to the conspiracy fire was the Vatican's handling of the aftermath. The lack of an autopsy was particularly scrutinized. While it's true that Vatican law traditionally forbade autopsies on popes, the circumstances seemed to call for an exception. The swift embalming of the body further raised eyebrows, with some claiming it was done to destroy evidence of foul play.

. . .

The theories gained traction in the public imagination, spawning books, documentaries, and even fictional adaptations. They tapped into a deep-seated fascination with Vatican secrets and the sometimes-opaque workings of one of the world's oldest institutions.

Yet for all the speculation, there were those who sought to debunk the murder theories. Journalists and researchers pored over the available evidence, interviewing witnesses and examining medical records. Many concluded that while the Vatican had indeed mishandled the situation, there was no evidence of foul play.

These investigations painted a different picture: that of a man with a history of health problems thrust into an immensely stressful role. John Paul I had suffered from low blood pressure and had been on medication for years. The sudden transition from a relatively quiet life as a cardinal to the demands of the papacy had likely taken a severe toll on his health.

Moreover, the pope's personal habits may have contributed to his demise. He was known to be a heavy smoker and had a family history of heart problems. The stress of his new role, combined with these risk factors, could easily explain a sudden heart attack.

As for the inconsistencies in the Vatican's account, these were attributed more to bureaucratic confusion and a desire to maintain dignity than to any sinister plot. The initial reluctance to admit that a nun had discovered the body, for instance, was explained as stemming from traditional Vatican protocols rather than an attempt at deception.

Despite these rational explanations, the mystery surrounding John Paul I's death has persisted. It speaks to a broader fascination with the papacy and the secretive nature of the Vatican. The idea that dark forces might be at work behind the scenes of one of the world's most revered institutions holds a powerful allure.

In recent years, efforts have been made to shed more light on John Paul I's life and death. The Vatican has opened its archives, allowing researchers to examine documents related to his brief papacy. These records have largely supported the official account of natural causes, though they've done little to quell the most determined conspiracy theorists.

. . .

The legacy of John Paul I extends beyond the circumstances of his death. His brief papacy, while not long enough to enact significant changes, did set a tone of humility and accessibility that would influence his successors. The "Smiling Pope" is remembered for his warmth and his desire to make the Church more responsive to the needs of ordinary people.

In 2017, Pope Francis approved the advancement of John Paul I's cause for sainthood, recognizing him as Venerable. This process has led to renewed interest in his life and teachings, shifting focus somewhat from the circumstances of his death to the impact of his life.

Yet the mystery endures. It serves as a reminder of the power of unanswered questions, of the human tendency to seek patterns and explanations in the face of the unexpected. The death of John Paul I, whether natural or not, underscores the complex interplay between faith, power, and human frailty.

In the end, what remains is the image of a man who, for 33 brief days, sat at the pinnacle of one of the world's most powerful institutions. A man who smiled warmly at the crowds in St. Peter's Square, who spoke of a Church more attuned to the needs of the poor, who dared to imagine change in an institution resistant to it.

Whether John Paul I died of natural causes or fell victim to a sinister plot, his story continues to captivate. It reminds us of the enduring mysteries that lie at the heart of human institutions, even those cloaked in divine authority. It speaks to our fascination with power and vulnerability, with the seen and the unseen forces that shape our world.

As the years pass and memories fade, the 33-day papacy of John Paul I remains a moment frozen in time. A brief flash of warmth and promise, extinguished all too soon, leaving behind questions that may never be fully answered. In that uncertainty lies the enduring power of his story, a testament to the complexities of faith, power, and human nature that continue to shape our world.

15

THE LEGEND OF THE TALKING STATUES

Stones have long memories, they say, but in Rome, they have voices too. For centuries, a handful of weathered statues scattered throughout the Eternal City have served as the unlikely mouthpieces for the people's discontent, wit, and rebellion. These are the talking statues of Rome, silent sentinels that have spoken volumes about power, corruption, and the indomitable spirit of satire.

The story begins in 1501, when workers unearthed a badly damaged ancient statue near the Piazza Navona. This battered remnant of a Hellenistic sculpture, possibly depicting the Greek hero Menelaus, might have been destined for obscurity. Instead, it became the most famous gossip in Rome.

.   .   .

Someone – history doesn't record who – decided to name
the statue Pasquino. Perhaps it was after a local school-
master known for his sharp tongue, or a barber whose
shop was a hotbed of neighborhood gossip. Whatever the
origin, the name stuck, and soon Pasquino found his
voice.

It started with a few lines of verse, scrawled on a scrap of
paper and pinned to the statue under the cover of darkness. The verses, known as pasquinades, were biting
satires aimed at the powerful – popes, cardinals, noble-
men. No one was safe from Pasquino's acid wit.

Word spread quickly. Soon, Romans were flocking to
Pasquino each morning to read the latest barbs. The
statue became a bulletin board for the city's frustrations
and a outlet for its satirical spirit. In an age before freedom
of the press, when criticizing the wrong person could lead
to exile or worse, Pasquino offered a veneer of anonymity.

The authorities were not amused. Pope Adrian VI, the
target of particularly vicious pasquinades, reportedly

considered having the statue thrown into the Tiber. But cooler heads prevailed, pointing out that Romans would likely say that Pasquino had become a martyr, "like Saint Peter."

Unable to silence Pasquino, the powers-that-be tried to co-opt him. During the Renaissance, it became fashionable for scholars to compose Latin epigrams and affix them to the statue, turning Pasquino into a sort of poetic competition. But the biting satires never stopped, merely hiding among the more erudite verses.

Pasquino's success inspired imitators. Other statues around Rome began to find their voices. There was Marforio, a reclining river god who often engaged in imaginary dialogues with Pasquino. Il Babuino, a statue of Silenus that Romans thought looked more like a baboon, joined the chorus. Madama Lucrezia, the only female among the talking statues, added her perspective. The Abate Luigi and Il Facchino rounded out the group.

Each statue developed its own personality and audience. Marforio, located near the Capitol, often spoke on political matters. Il Babuino, on the street that now bears his name, was a favorite of artists and bohemians. Madama Lucrezia, sitting in the Piazza di San Marco, was known for her gossip about the nobility.

The talking statues became a Roman institution, a unique form of social media centuries before the internet. They were a public forum where news was shared, scandals were exposed, and the powerful were held to account – all under the thin veil of anonymity provided by the cover of night.

During papal elections, the statues were particularly vocal. The transition of power was a tense time in Rome, and the pasquinades offered a release valve for public anxiety and speculation. Some of the most famous pasquinades from this period were sharp commentaries on the corruption of the Church.

One famous exchange, likely apocryphal but telling nonetheless, had Marforio asking Pasquino, "Why are the carriages of the cardinals covered in velvet and silk, while the carriage of Jesus in the Eucharist procession is so plain?" Pasquino's cutting reply: "Jesus is humble and poor, but the cardinals are neither."

. . .

The practice wasn't limited to locals. Visitors to Rome, including famous writers and artists, would sometimes leave their own contributions. The statues became a must-see attraction, a way to take the pulse of the city and perhaps add one's own voice to the chorus.

As centuries passed, the talking statues adapted to changing times. During the French occupation of Rome in the late 18th century, they became a focus of resistance, voicing the people's resentment of foreign rule. In the lead-up to Italian unification, they spoke of national aspirations and critiqued the papal government's opposition to the Risorgimento.

The advent of newspapers and greater press freedom in the 19th century might have spelled the end for the talking statues, but they proved resilient. Even as other outlets for public opinion emerged, Romans continued to turn to their stone confidants. During World War II, the statues once again became a medium for resistance, this time against the fascist regime and the German occupation.

In the post-war period, the practice began to fade. The rapid pace of modern life and new forms of communication made the nightly ritual of pinning notes to statues seem quaint. By the 1960s, the talking statues had fallen largely silent.

Yet, like so much in Rome, they never truly disappeared. In times of particular political turmoil or public frustration, papers would once again appear on Pasquino or his colleagues. The tradition might lie dormant, but it was never forgotten.

Today, the talking statues stand as a testament to Rome's enduring spirit of satire and resistance. Pasquino, still in his spot near the Piazza Navona, occasionally receives a modern pasquinade. Tourists seek out the statues, drawn by their unique place in the city's history.

The legacy of the talking statues extends beyond Rome. The term "pasquinade" entered the English language as a synonym for a lampoon or satirical criticism. The idea of anonymous public commentary, so central to the internet age, finds an early precedent in these weather-worn figures.

. . .

As Rome grapples with 21st-century challenges, from overtourism to political corruption, some have called for a revival of the talking statues tradition. In an age of online echo chambers and algorithmic news feeds, they argue, there's something powerful about physical spaces for public discourse.

Whether or not Pasquino and his fellow statues find their voices again, their story remains a powerful reminder of the enduring human need for free expression. In the face of power, be it papal, royal, or democratic, people will always find ways to speak truth to authority – even if they have to put words in the mouths of statues to do so.

The talking statues of Rome stand as silent witnesses to centuries of history, their weathered surfaces holding the echoes of countless voices. They remind us that rebellion can take many forms, that humor can be a powerful weapon against oppression, and that even in the darkest times, people will find ways to make themselves heard.

In a city where every stone seems to tell a story, these statues have more tales to tell than most. They speak of a Rome beyond the guidebooks, a city of wit and resistance, where even the sculptures have learned to talk back. As long as there are injustices to critique and follies to mock, one suspects that Pasquino and his friends will always have something to say.

16

THE VANISHING FONTANA DELLE TARTARUGHE

Water has always been Rome's lifeblood, and its fountains are the jewels that adorn the city's timeworn streets. Among these, the Fontana delle Tartarughe, or Turtle Fountain, stands out as a masterpiece of whimsy and grace. Nestled in the intimate Piazza Mattei, this Renaissance gem tells a story of art, love, and the enduring spirit of a city that has reinvented itself countless times.

The tale of the Turtle Fountain begins in the late 16th century, a time when Rome was shaking off the dust of the Middle Ages and embracing the artistic fervor of the Renaissance. In 1581, Duke Muzio Mattei, a scion of one of Rome's noble families, commissioned a new fountain to grace the square outside his palazzo. The task fell to

Giacomo della Porta, an architect whose works would come to define the face of Baroque Rome.

Della Porta envisioned a fountain that would be both a public utility and a work of art. He designed a square basin with an upper bowl, supported by four marble shells. But it was the sculptor Taddeo Landini who breathed life into the fountain, creating four bronze ephebes – youthful male figures – that would become its defining feature.

These bronze youths, poised with elegant contrapposto, were originally meant to be accompanied by dolphins. Each ephebe would rest one foot on a dolphin's back, creating a dynamic composition of man and beast. But Rome, ever a city of practical challenges, had other plans.

The fountain was to be fed by the Acqua Vergine, an ancient aqueduct restored to glory during the Renaissance. However, the water pressure proved insufficient to support jets from multiple dolphins. In a decision that would alter the fountain's design, four of the eight planned dolphins were removed and repurposed for another fountain at the Piazza della Chiesa Nuova.

.   .   .

This change left the upper part of the fountain feeling unfinished, a rare flaw in the meticulous world of Renaissance design. For decades, the Turtle Fountain stood in this incomplete state, admired for its beauty but always hinting at something missing.

The solution came in 1658, during the reign of Pope Alexander VII. In a stroke of artistic genius – variously attributed to the great Gian Lorenzo Bernini or his contemporary Andrea Sacchi – four bronze turtles were added to the fountain's upper basin. These small creatures, positioned as if climbing into the water, filled the visual gap left by the missing dolphins and added a touch of whimsy to the classical design.

The addition of the turtles transformed the fountain. What had been a beautiful but conventional Renaissance work became something unique – a playful blend of the elegant and the unexpected. The turtles, with their unhurried climb towards the water, seemed to capture something of Rome's own character: a city where the grand and the humble, the ancient and the modern, coexist in perpetual, charming contradiction.

· · ·

But the story of the Turtle Fountain doesn't end with its completion. Over the centuries, it has accumulated layers of legend and lore, becoming as much a part of Rome's mythology as its physical landscape.

The most beloved tale associated with the fountain speaks to the eternal Roman themes of love, pride, and the power of art to change fortunes. According to this legend, Duke Mattei was a notorious gambler who had lost his entire fortune in a single night of reckless betting. When his prospective father-in-law heard of this disaster, he immediately called off the engagement, unwilling to tie his daughter's fate to that of a ruined man.

Desperate to salvage both his reputation and his romance, Mattei hatched an audacious plan. He vowed to build a magnificent fountain overnight, right outside his palazzo. If he could accomplish this feat, surely it would prove his resourcefulness and worth as a son-in-law.

The story goes that Mattei employed an army of artisans who worked through the night in a frenzy of creativity. As dawn broke, the Turtle Fountain stood complete, a testament to Mattei's determination and the skill of Roman craftsmen. When the duke invited his would-be bride and her father to look out the window, they were astounded by the beautiful fountain that seemed to have sprung up from nowhere.

Impressed by this display of wealth and influence, the father relented, and the marriage went ahead as planned. It's a charming tale, one that captures the romantic spirit of Renaissance Rome. Of course, like many such legends, it wilts under historical scrutiny – the fountain and the Mattei Palace were built decades apart. But in Rome, a good story often trumps mere facts.

The real history of the fountain, while less dramatic, is no less intriguing. Its location in what was once the heart of Rome's Jewish Ghetto speaks to the complex social fabric of the city. For centuries, this area was a place of confinement and persecution for Rome's Jewish community. The fountain, with its beauty and practicality, served as a meeting point and a rare touch of elegance in an often-neglected part of the city.

Over time, the Turtle Fountain became more than just a work of art – it became a symbol of the neighborhood and a beloved landmark for all Romans. But this very fame also brought challenges. The fountain's bronze elements, particularly the charming turtles, proved irresistible to thieves and vandals.

In 1979, Romans woke to shocking news: one of the turtles had been stolen in the night. The audacity of the theft sparked outrage and a citywide search. Though the missing turtle was never recovered, the incident led to increased protection for the fountain. The remaining original turtles were moved to the safety of the Capitoline Museums, replaced on the fountain by exact replicas.

This modern chapter in the fountain's history highlights the ongoing challenge of preserving Rome's artistic heritage in a living, changing city. It's a delicate balance between allowing public access to art and protecting it for future generations.

Today, the Turtle Fountain continues to delight visitors and locals alike. Its modest scale and tucked-away location make discovering it feel like uncovering a secret, a hidden gem in a city full of more famous monuments. The play of water over bronze and stone, the graceful poses of the ephebes, and the whimsical climb of the turtles create a scene of timeless charm.

· · ·

But beyond its aesthetic appeal, the Turtle Fountain embodies something essential about Rome itself. It's a testament to the city's ability to adapt and evolve, to take the unfinished or imperfect and transform it into something magical. The addition of the turtles to solve a design flaw mirrors Rome's own history of building upon its past, layer upon layer, each generation adding its own touch to the eternal city.

As visitors pause by the fountain, perhaps to toss a coin or simply to admire its beauty, they become part of this ongoing story. In the quiet splash of water and the glint of sunlight on bronze, they can hear echoes of Renaissance artists at work, of secret midnight labors, of centuries of Roman life flowing past. The Turtle Fountain stands as a reminder that in Rome, every corner holds a story, every stone has a tale to tell – if only we take the time to listen.

17

THE HAUNTING OF PALAZZO DORIA PAMPHILJ

Rome has always been a city of whispers, where the past refuses to stay buried and the lines between history and legend blur. Among its many tales of intrigue and mystery, few are as captivating as the story of Olimpia Maidalchini Pamphilj, the woman known as "La Papessa" - the She-Pope. Her life was a testament to ambition and cunning, and her death... well, that's where the real story begins.

Born in 1591 in Viterbo, a small town north of Rome, Olimpia seemed destined for an unremarkable life. But fate - and her own fierce determination - had other plans. Widowed young and left with a substantial fortune, she set her sights on the corridors of power in Rome. Her second marriage to Pamphilio Pamphilj, brother of the future Pope Innocent X, was her ticket into the heart of the Vatican.

From the moment she arrived in Rome, Olimpia made waves. She was intelligent, ambitious, and utterly ruthless. In a world dominated by men, she carved out a place for herself through sheer force of will. When her brother-in-law ascended to the papal throne in 1644, Olimpia saw her chance and seized it with both hands.

Soon, whispers began to circulate through Rome's winding streets. Olimpia, they said, was the real power behind the papal throne. She controlled the Vatican's finances, influenced political decisions, and even, some dared to suggest, shared the Pope's bed. The Romans, never shy about expressing their opinions, gave her a new title: "La Papessa" - the She-Pope.

Olimpia's rise to power was as swift as it was controversial. Appointed Minister of Finance and the Streets of Rome, she used her position to amass an enormous fortune. Heavy taxes were imposed, bribes were accepted, and those who crossed her found themselves quickly out of favor. The people of Rome seethed, but Olimpia seemed untouchable.

. . .

Yet even as she accumulated wealth and power, Olimpia was not content to be merely rich. She had grander ambitions. Under her influence, Rome underwent a transformation. The Piazza Navona, where she made her home, became a showcase of Baroque splendor. The crowning jewel was the Fontana dei Quattro Fiumi, designed by the great Gian Lorenzo Bernini - a project that bore Olimpia's fingerprints in every sculpted detail.

Olimpia's patronage extended beyond architecture. She commissioned works from some of the greatest artists of the age, including Diego Velázquez, whose portrait of Innocent X hangs to this day in the Palazzo Doria Pamphilj. The palace itself, a sprawling testament to the family's wealth and influence, grew ever more opulent under her guidance.

But for all her contributions to Rome's beauty, Olimpia was far from beloved. The streets buzzed with stories of her greed, her manipulation, her insatiable appetite for power. Satirical verses, known as pasquinades, appeared on statues throughout the city, mocking "La Papessa" and accusing her of every sin imaginable. Some depicted her as a witch, others as the true ruler of Rome, with the Pope as nothing more than her puppet.

Olimpia weathered these storms of public opinion with characteristic steel. She had not come this far, risen so high, to be brought low by the mutterings of the common people. As long as she had the Pope's ear - and his heart - she was untouchable.

But time, that great equalizer, was not on Olimpia's side. As the 1650s wore on, Pope Innocent X's health began to fail. Olimpia, ever the pragmatist, began to prepare for the inevitable. She knew that once her protector was gone, her enemies would waste no time in seeking revenge.

In January 1655, as the Pope lay on his deathbed, Rome held its breath. For days, the city was gripped by an eerie quiet, broken only by the tolling of church bells and the whispered prayers of the faithful. And then, on a cold winter's night, something extraordinary happened.

A black carriage was seen racing through the streets of Rome, heading for the Porta Portese. Witnesses swore they saw Olimpia herself at the reins, her face a mask of determination. Behind her, the carriage groaned under the weight of two enormous chests, said to be filled with gold and priceless treasures looted from the Vatican coffers.

As the carriage clattered across the Ponte Sisto bridge, those who saw it were struck by a sense of otherworldly dread. The horses seemed to breathe fire, their eyes glowing red in the darkness. And Olimpia, her hair streaming behind her like a battle standard, let out a laugh that echoed through the night - a sound of triumph and defiance.

By morning, she was gone. Pope Innocent X died soon after, and with him died Olimpia's hold on power. She retreated to her estate in San Martino al Cimino, where she lived out her days in relative obscurity. When the plague swept through Italy in 1657, it claimed Olimpia as one of its victims, a quiet end for a woman who had lived such a tumultuous life.

But death, it seemed, was not the end of Olimpia's story.

. . .

It began with whispers, as so many things in Rome do. People walking near the Palazzo Doria Pamphilj late at night reported strange sights and sounds. The clip-clop of phantom hooves on cobblestones. The creak of carriage wheels where no carriage could be seen. And sometimes, on the darkest nights, the sound of a woman's laughter, tinged with madness and triumph.

Soon, the stories spread. Olimpia, they said, had returned to haunt the city she once ruled. Her ghost was seen riding her black carriage across the Ponte Sisto, the very route she had taken on that fateful night in 1655. Some claimed to see her clutching her chests of gold, her eyes burning with the same ambition that had driven her in life.

The hauntings were not confined to the bridge. Around the Piazza Navona, where Olimpia had made her home, people reported feeling sudden chills, even on the warmest summer nights. Shadows seemed to move of their own accord, and more than one person swore they had seen a figure in 17th-century dress standing at a window of the Palazzo Doria Pamphilj, only for it to vanish when they looked again.

. . .

These ghostly apparitions were accompanied by strange phenomena. Lights flickered in empty rooms of the palace. Objects moved on their own. Visitors to the gallery that housed Olimpia's portrait sometimes felt an unseen presence watching them, a sensation so unsettling that more than one person had fled the room in terror.

The legend of Olimpia's ghost grew, taking on a life of its own. It was said that those who saw her spectral carriage were struck with a paralyzing fear, unable to move or cry out as the ghostly procession passed. Others claimed that to hear Olimpia's phantom laughter was to invite misfortune, a curse that could last for years.

Some saw these hauntings as Olimpia's punishment, her spirit doomed to relive her flight from Rome for all eternity. Others believed it was an act of defiance, a refusal to relinquish her hold on the city even in death. Whatever the truth, the ghost of "La Papessa" became as much a part of Rome's folklore as the she-wolf that nursed Romulus and Remus.

Today, the Palazzo Doria Pamphilj stands as a museum, its halls filled with priceless artworks collected over centuries. Visitors can see Velázquez's famous portrait of

Pope Innocent X, his shrewd eyes seeming to follow them around the room. They can admire the bust of Olimpia herself, carved by Alessandro Algardi, capturing forever the strength and determination that defined her.

But for all the beauty on display, it's the unseen that draws many to the palace. They come hoping for a glimpse of the infamous "La Papessa," for a brush with the supernatural that will confirm the legends they've heard. Most leave disappointed, having experienced nothing more than the quiet reverence of a great art collection.

Yet sometimes, as the sun sets and shadows lengthen across the Piazza Navona, a chill wind blows through the square. The clip-clop of hooves echoes off ancient stones, and for a moment, just a moment, one might catch a glimpse of a black carriage racing by, driven by a woman whose ambition and will were powerful enough to outlast death itself.

The story of Olimpia Maidalchini Pamphilj is more than just a ghost story. It's a tale of power, ambition, and the marks we leave on the world - for good or ill. In life, she shaped Rome through her patronage and her politics. In death, she became part of the city's rich mythology, a cautionary tale and a source of fascination in equal measure.

Whether one believes in ghosts or not, the legend of Olimpia serves as a reminder of Rome's complex history, where the sacred and the profane, the historical and the mythical, have always existed side by side. Her story continues to captivate, a testament to the enduring power of ambition and the way in which our actions in life can echo long after we're gone.

So the next time you find yourself in Rome, walking the moonlit streets near the Palazzo Doria Pamphilj, keep your eyes and ears open. You never know when you might encounter the ghost of "La Papessa," still racing through the eternal city, forever seeking power, forever fleeing judgment, a woman who refused to be forgotten by history or contained by the grave.

18

THE ENIGMATIC PYRAMID OF CESTIUS

Amidst the domes, arches, and columns that define Rome's skyline, a sharp triangular form pierces the sky. It's not a mirage or a trick of the light, but a genuine pyramid, standing proudly near the Porta San Paolo. This is the Pyramid of Cestius, a monument that has puzzled and fascinated visitors for two millennia.

To understand how this Egyptian-style tomb came to be built in Rome, we must travel back to the tumultuous final years of the Roman Republic. The year is 12 BC, and Rome is still basking in the afterglow of its conquest of Egypt. The streets buzz with talk of the exotic treasures and strange customs of this ancient land. Obelisks rise in the forums, and the cult of Isis gains followers among the Roman elite.

Enter Gaius Cestius Epulo, a man of wealth and status. As a member of the Septemviri Epulonum, a prestigious college of priests responsible for organizing religious feasts, Cestius moved in the highest circles of Roman society. Yet for all his importance in life, it's in death that Cestius would make his most lasting mark on the Eternal City.

What possessed Cestius to commission a pyramid as his final resting place? Was it a fascination with all things Egyptian, sparked by Rome's recent conquest? Or perhaps a desire to stand out from his peers, even in death? The true reasons are lost to time, but the result of his decision still looms over Rome today.

Construction of the pyramid began shortly after Cestius' death. His will was clear: the monument was to be completed within 330 days, or his heirs would face severe penalties. One can imagine the frantic activity at the building site as workers raced against time to fulfill the peculiar last wish of their wealthy patron.

. . .

The pyramid rose quickly, its core of brick-faced concrete covered with gleaming slabs of Carrara marble. At 36.4 meters (119 feet) high, with a square base of 29.6 meters (97 feet) per side, it was an imposing sight. The sharp 43-degree angle of its sides created a more acute point than the pyramids of Giza, perhaps due to Roman engineers working from descriptions rather than first-hand observations of the Egyptian originals.

As the pyramid neared completion, artisans carved inscriptions into its marble facing. These words, still visible today, tell us what little we know about Cestius: his name, his priestly title, and the speed with which his tomb was built. They stand as Cestius' last boast, a final declaration of his importance to a world he was leaving behind.

Inside the pyramid, a small burial chamber was prepared. Unlike the labyrinthine interiors of its Egyptian counterparts, the Pyramid of Cestius contained just a single, modest room. The walls were adorned with frescoes depicting female figures and scenes that have long since faded to mere shadows. Whatever treasures might have accompanied Cestius on his journey to the afterlife have been lost to time and tomb robbers.

. . .

With its completion, the Pyramid of Cestius joined the mausoleums and monuments lining the roads leading out of Rome. It must have been a startling sight to travelers, this slice of Egypt rising unexpectedly from the Italian landscape. Yet strangely, contemporary writers barely mentioned it. Perhaps in a city constantly reinventing itself, even a pyramid could fail to cause much of a stir.

As centuries passed, Rome changed around the pyramid. The Republic gave way to Empire, paganism to Christianity, ancient glory to medieval decay. Through it all, Cestius' tomb endured. Its survival is due in part to a stroke of luck: when Emperor Aurelian ordered new walls built to defend Rome in the 3rd century AD, the pyramid was incorporated into their structure. This quirk of urban planning preserved the monument, protecting it from the fate that befell many ancient buildings, which were dismantled for their stone.

The Middle Ages draped a cloak of mystery over the pyramid. As knowledge of Rome's imperial past faded, legends grew to explain the strange monument. It was said to be the tomb of Remus, brother of Rome's founder Romulus. Others claimed it housed the remains of the Biblical tribunes Simeon and Levi. These tales speak to

installation of new lighting, allowing the pyramid to shine at night as a beacon of Rome's multi-layered history.

Today, the Pyramid of Cestius stands as a testament to the enduring allure of ancient Egypt and the complex cultural exchanges of the ancient world. It reminds us that Rome, for all its own remarkable achievements, was also a city that absorbed and reinterpreted influences from across its vast empire.

Visitors who stand before the pyramid today might ponder the same questions that have intrigued observers for centuries. What drove Cestius to choose this alien form for his tomb? Did he see himself as a Roman pharaoh, or was he simply a man determined to be remembered? And how would he feel knowing that his monument has long outlasted any memory of his deeds in life?

Perhaps the greatest irony of the Pyramid of Cestius is that while it has preserved Cestius' name through the ages, it tells us almost nothing about the man himself. He remains an enigma, defined only by his unusual choice of final resting place. In this, the pyramid serves as a poignant reminder of the capricious nature of legacy and remembrance.

As Rome continues to evolve around it, the Pyramid of Cestius maintains its silent vigil. It stands as a bridge between cultures, a fusion of Egyptian form and Roman engineering. More than that, it's a symbol of the human desire to leave a mark on the world, to create something that will outlast us and keep our names alive long after we're gone.

In the end, the Pyramid of Cestius is more than just an architectural oddity or a historical curiosity. It's a monument to the power of an idea, to the allure of the exotic, and to the eternal human quest for immortality. As long as it stands, a piece of Egypt in the heart of Rome, it will continue to inspire wonder, spark imagination, and connect us to the dreams and ambitions of those who came before us.

19

THE LEGEND OF THE DEVIL'S FOOTPRINT

arble floors whisper ancient secrets in the vast expanse of the Basilica di San Paolo fuori le Mura. Among the gleaming columns and gilded mosaics, a small, unassuming mark catches the eye of those who know where to look. It's not an artist's signature or a mason's mistake, but something far more sinister - the alleged footprint of the Devil himself.

The story of this infernal imprint begins in the early 4th century when Emperor Constantine I ordered the construction of a grand basilica over the burial site of St. Paul the Apostle. As the walls rose and the altar took shape, word spread through Rome of the magnificent church being built to honor one of Christianity's most revered figures.

But not everyone, it seems, was pleased with this development.

Legend has it that one moonless night, as the basilica neared completion, a dark figure slipped past the slumbering guards. This was no common thief or curious onlooker, but Satan himself, drawn by jealousy and rage to this monument of faith. His plan was simple: destroy the basilica before it could be consecrated, dealing a crushing blow to the growing Christian community in Rome.

As the Devil crept towards the altar, his cloven hooves clicking softly on the marble floor, he was suddenly confronted by a blinding light. There, before him, stood the spectral figure of St. Paul, guardian of the basilica even in death. The two adversaries faced each other in the silent church, mortal enemies locked in an age-old battle.

What words were exchanged, what cosmic threats made, we'll never know. But as the light faded and St. Paul's spirit retreated, the Devil found himself thwarted, unable to carry out his destructive mission. In a fit of impotent rage, he stamped his foot so hard on the marble floor that he left a deep, permanent impression - a mark of his failure and a testament to the power of faith.

This tale, passed down through generations of Romans, pilgrims, and priests, offers a tantalizing blend of the miraculous and the macabre. It speaks to the eternal struggle between good and evil, casting the basilica not just as a place of worship, but as a battlefield in a cosmic war.

But what of the footprint itself? Those who've seen it describe an impression larger than a human foot, with an oddly elongated shape and marks that could be interpreted as claws. Skeptics might point out that marble, being a metamorphic rock, can develop natural irregularities. Yet for believers, the very existence of this mark, so close to the sacred altar, is proof enough of its infernal origin.

The legend of the Devil's footprint is just one thread in the rich tapestry of lore surrounding the Basilica di San Paolo fuori le Mura. This immense church, second only to

St. Peter's in size, has weathered centuries of triumph and tragedy. Its walls have echoed with the prayers of countless pilgrims, the chants of monks, and the pronouncements of popes.

Yet even as it stood as a beacon of faith, the basilica was not immune to disaster. In 1823, a fire ravaged the ancient structure, reducing much of it to ashes. The blaze, ironically started by a careless workman's unattended brazier, seemed to fulfill the destructive mission the Devil had failed to accomplish centuries before.

But from these ashes, the basilica rose again. Pope Leo XII called on the Catholic world to contribute to its reconstruction, and donations poured in from across the globe. Skilled artisans and architects labored to recreate the basilica's former glory, melding ancient designs with modern techniques.

Remarkably, amidst the devastation, certain elements of the old basilica survived. The apse with its priceless mosaics emerged largely unscathed, as did the triumphal arch. And there, near the altar, the Devil's footprint remained, untouched by the flames that had consumed so much around it.

. . .

For some, this survival was yet another miracle, a sign of divine protection extending even to this mark of evil, preserving it as a reminder of faith's triumph. Others saw it as proof of the footprint's supernatural origin - surely no mere imperfection in the stone could have withstood such an inferno.

Today, visitors to the basilica find themselves immersed in a space that bridges centuries. The soaring nave, lined with 80 granite columns, leads the eye inevitably to the papal altar and the triumphal arch beyond. Above, a mosaic of Christ looks down in eternal benediction, flanked by the symbols of the four evangelists.

Yet even amidst such grandeur, many find their gaze drawn to that small, strange mark on the floor. They pause, ponder, perhaps offer a silent prayer. Some even attempt to fit their own foot into the impression, as if trying to measure themselves against the forces of darkness.

The Devil's footprint is more than just a curiosity or a photo opportunity. It serves as a physical reminder of the spiritual battles that have shaped Rome's history. In a city where the sacred and the profane have always coexisted, where pagan temples became Christian churches and ancient myths blended with new beliefs, this mark embodies the constant interplay between light and shadow.

But the footprint is not the only relic that draws pilgrims to San Paolo fuori le Mura. Beneath the papal altar lies the tomb of St. Paul himself, a destination for countless faithful over the centuries. In 2006, Vatican archaeologists confirmed the presence of a sarcophagus believed to contain the apostle's remains, adding scientific weight to centuries of tradition.

Another treasured relic is the chain said to have bound Paul during his imprisonment in Rome. Displayed in a golden reliquary, these links of iron serve as a tangible connection to the early days of Christianity, when faith often came at the cost of freedom or even life.

As one wanders the basilica, other stories emerge from its art and architecture. The giant Easter candlestick, standing over 5 meters tall, tells the story of Christ's passion and resurrection in intricate marble relief. The portraits of every pope from St. Peter to Francis line the upper walls, a visual timeline of the Church's history.

In the peaceful cloister, with its delicately carved twin columns and serene garden, one finds a space for quiet contemplation. Here, it's easy to imagine generations of monks walking in silent meditation, pondering the mysteries of faith - perhaps even the mystery of that devilish mark near the altar.

The Basilica di San Paolo fuori le Mura stands as a testament to the resilience of faith and the power of human creativity. From its foundations on the site of the apostle's tomb to its soaring dome, it embodies the story of Christianity in Rome. It has weathered fires and earthquakes, survived wars and the fall of empires, always rising again, always calling the faithful to prayer.

And through it all, that curious footprint has remained, a small imperfection in the vast perfection of the basilica. It reminds us that even in the holiest of places, the shadows of doubt and fear can intrude. Yet it also stands as proof that these shadows can be overcome, that faith can triumph over the darkest of forces.

. . .

As night falls and the last visitors leave, the basilica grows quiet. And there, near the altar, a patch of moonlight might just illuminate a strange depression in the marble floor - the spot where, if the legends are to be believed, the Devil himself once stood and was defeated.

The Devil's footprint in San Paolo fuori le Mura is a tale that continues to captivate. It speaks to our fascination with the battle between good and evil, our need to find meaning in the unexplained, and our eternal hope that, in the end, light will always triumph over darkness.

Whether seen as literal truth, metaphorical lesson, or mere superstition, the legend of the Devil's footprint adds another layer to the rich history of this ancient basilica. It reminds us that faith is not just about grand gestures and mighty edifices, but also about the small marks left behind - the imprints, both physical and spiritual, that tell the story of our struggles and our triumphs.

20

THE GHOSTLY LEGIONS OF VIA APPIA

The stones of the Appian Way have witnessed the march of history for over two millennia. This ancient Roman road, stretching from the capital to the southern reaches of the Italian peninsula, has borne the weight of countless travelers, from humble merchants to conquering armies. But some say that not all who walk this storied path are of flesh and blood. For centuries, tales have persisted of spectral legions, Roman soldiers forever bound to the road they once patrolled in life.

Built in 312 BC under the direction of Appius Claudius Caecus, the Via Appia Antica was more than just a road. It was an artery of empire, a conduit for Rome's inexorable expansion southward. Its construction was a feat of engineering that defied the limits of its time. Massive stones were laid with precision, creating a surface so smooth and durable that parts of it remain intact to this day.

As Rome grew, so did the Appian Way. It stretched further south, eventually reaching Brundisium (modern-day Brindisi), a vital port for trade and military operations in the eastern Mediterranean. The road became a symbol of Roman power and ingenuity, a lifeline that connected the heart of the empire to its furthest reaches.

But the Via Appia was more than just a thoroughfare for the living. In keeping with Roman custom, it also became a final resting place for the dead. Tombs and mausoleums sprang up along its length, from modest markers to grand monuments. The road became a necropolis, a city of the dead that mirrored the bustling world of the living that passed between them.

It's perhaps no surprise, then, that such a place should become the subject of ghostly tales. The first whispers of spectral legions came during the tumultuous years of the late Roman Empire. As barbarian invasions threatened and the once-invincible legions faltered, soldiers reported strange sightings along the moonlit road. They spoke of transparent figures in ancient armor, marching in perfect formation, their feet making no sound on the well-worn stones.

At first, these tales were dismissed as the product of tired minds and nervous dispositions. But as the years passed and the empire crumbled, the stories persisted. Travelers would return to Rome with accounts of entire ghostly cohorts seen in the dead of night, their standards held high and their faces set with grim determination.

One particularly chilling account comes from the 6th century, just before the Gothic Wars that would devastate Italy. A group of merchants, traveling south to trade in the Byzantine-held territories, made camp for the night along the Appian Way. As the moon rose, they were startled by the sound of marching feet. To their amazement, they saw a column of soldiers approaching, their armor gleaming despite the lack of any visible light source.

The merchants hid, fearing these might be Gothic raiders. But as the column passed, they realized they could see through the bodies of the soldiers to the tombs behind them. The ghostly legion marched on, oblivious to the trembling witnesses, before fading into the night mists.

．．．

This encounter sparked a flurry of similar reports. Some claimed to have seen the ghost of Julius Caesar himself, leading his loyal troops on one final march. Others spoke of spectral battles fought between long-dead armies, their clash of arms silent but their movements all too real.

As the centuries passed, the legend of the Appian Way's ghosts grew and evolved. During the Renaissance, as interest in Rome's ancient past was rekindled, the road became a popular subject for artists and writers. They were drawn not just to its historical significance, but to the air of mystery and supernatural dread that had come to surround it.

One recurring element in these tales was the idea of unfinished business. Many believed that the ghostly soldiers were the spirits of those who had died far from home, their bodies buried in foreign soil. The Appian Way, which had carried them to war in life, became their eternal path in death, a road that led forever onward but never to rest.

．．．

This concept resonated particularly strongly in the context of Rome's many wars. The Appian Way had seen the march of legions bound for conflicts in Greece, North Africa, and the East. How many of those soldiers, it was wondered, had never returned? How many still sought, in some spectral way, to complete their final journey home?

The road's association with death was further cemented by one of the grimmest episodes in Roman history. In 71 BC, following the suppression of Spartacus' slave revolt, the Roman general Crassus ordered the crucifixion of 6,000 captured rebels along the Appian Way. For miles, the road was lined with crosses, a brutal demonstration of Rome's power and a warning to any who would challenge it.

This mass execution left a psychic scar on the landscape. In the centuries that followed, travelers reported seeing the ghosts of the crucified, their spectral forms still hanging from invisible crosses. Others claimed to hear agonized moans carried on the wind, or to feel an oppressive sense of sorrow and anger in certain stretches of the road.

· · ·

The ghostly legends of the Appian Way reached beyond pagan Rome and into the Christian era. As the new faith spread, the road's catacombs became a refuge for early Christians, hiding from persecution and burying their dead. These underground chambers, with their winding passages and countless tombs, spawned their own supernatural tales.

Some spoke of ghostly congregations, gathering in the depths of the earth to celebrate eternal mass. Others reported encounters with spectral martyrs, their forms radiating an unearthly light. The lines between Christian miracle and pagan haunting blurred, creating a unique folklore that reflected Rome's complex spiritual history.

As the Middle Ages gave way to the modern era, the Appian Way's ghostly reputation only grew. Tourists and pilgrims alike would time their travels to avoid being on the road after dark. Those forced to make night journeys would arm themselves with prayers and talismans, hoping to ward off any supernatural encounters.

Yet for every traveler who feared the road's ghosts, there was another who sought them out. The 18th and 19th centuries saw a surge of interest in the supernatural, and the Appian Way became a prime destination for ghost-hunters and thrill-seekers. Armed with early cameras and spirit boxes, these investigators hoped to capture proof of the afterlife on the ancient stones of the Via Appia.

While hard evidence remained elusive, the steady stream of reported encounters kept the legend alive. Some claimed to have captured ghostly figures in their photographs, while others reported sudden and inexplicable equipment failures when trying to document their experiences. The road, it seemed, was reluctant to give up its secrets.

In the 20th century, as archaeology and historical preservation efforts intensified, new layers were added to the Appian Way's supernatural lore. Excavations uncovered long-forgotten tombs and artifacts, each find sparking new ghostly tales. Workers reported strange occurrences: tools moving on their own, unexplained cold spots, and the sensation of being watched by unseen eyes.

One particularly notable incident occurred in the 1960s, when a team of archaeologists was conducting a night survey of a newly discovered mausoleum. As they worked, they began to hear the distinct sound of marching feet and clanking armor. The noise grew louder, seeming to approach from all directions at once. The team abandoned their equipment and fled, only to find the road empty and silent when they gathered the courage to return.

Today, the Appian Way stands as both a historical treasure and a supernatural enigma. By day, it's a popular tourist destination, its ancient pavements walked by visitors from around the world. But as night falls and the crowds thin, the road seems to hold its breath, as if waiting for its ghostly inhabitants to emerge once more.

Ghost tours now ply the Via Appia after dark, offering brave souls the chance to experience its eerie atmosphere for themselves. Guides recount the tales of spectral legions and ancient battles, while keeping a watchful eye for any unexplained phenomena. More often than not, the night passes without incident. But there are always a few who claim to have seen a flicker of movement in the shadows, or heard the faint echo of long-dead voices on the wind.

Whether one believes in ghosts or not, the legends of the Appian Way serve as a powerful reminder of the deep connections between place and memory. In its stones and its stories, we find a living link to the past, a way to touch the lives and deaths of those who came before us. The spectral legions, real or imagined, march on through history, forever bound to the road that once carried them to glory and to doom.

As Rome continues to evolve, the Appian Way remains a constant, a thread that connects the eternal city to its ancient roots. And on quiet nights, when the moon is high and the wind whispers through the ruins, one might still catch a glimpse of those ghostly soldiers, forever on the march to a destination they can never reach. Their eternal journey serves as a haunting testament to the enduring power of Rome's legacy, a reminder that some roads, once traveled, can never truly be left behind.

21

THE TREVI FOUNTAIN COINS

Water cascades over intricate baroque sculptures, the sound of coins plinking against the bottom of the pool barely audible above the rush. This is the Trevi Fountain, one of Rome's most iconic landmarks and the site of a curious modern ritual. Every day, thousands of visitors turn their backs to the fountain, coins in hand, and toss their spare change over their shoulders into the water. It's a simple act, but one loaded with hope, superstition, and a touch of magic.

The tradition of throwing coins into the Trevi Fountain is relatively young compared to the ancient monuments that surround it. The fountain itself, with its grand facade depicting Oceanus and his entourage, was completed in 1762. But it wasn't until the 1954 film "Three Coins in the Fountain" that the practice of coin-tossing really took off. The movie popularized the idea that throwing one coin ensures a return to Rome, two coins lead to new romance, and three coins guarantee marriage or divorce.

Today, it's estimated that over €3,000 worth of coins are thrown into the fountain every day, adding up to more than €1 million annually. But what happens to all that money? Where does it go? And why do people continue to participate in this ritual with such enthusiasm?

The answers to these questions reveal a fascinating intersection of tradition, charity, and urban legend. Each night, after the tourists have gone and the piazza grows quiet, a team of workers wades into the fountain. Armed with nets and vacuum hoses, they meticulously collect every coin tossed in over the course of the day. It's a necessary task - if left uncollected, the coins would eventually damage the fountain's delicate marble.

But this nightly collection is more than just maintenance. It's the first step in a process that transforms tourists' wishes into tangible good for the city. Since 2001, all the money collected from the Trevi Fountain has been donated to Caritas, a Catholic charity that operates throughout Rome. The funds support a supermarket for the city's needy, as well as various social programs aimed at helping Rome's most vulnerable residents.

It's a noble use for the fountain's bounty, but it hasn't always been this way. For years, the coins were a tempting target for thieves. The most famous of these was known as d'Artagnan, after the character from "The Three Muske-teers." For over 30 years, this modern-day Robin Hood would wade into the fountain at night, pocketing coins to supplement his meager pension. He became something of a local legend, evading capture time and again despite the authorities' best efforts.

The story of d'Artagnan highlights the complex relationship Romans have with the fountain and its coins. On one hand, there's a recognition that the money can do real good when properly collected and distributed. On the other, there's a sense that the coins represent the hopes and dreams of visitors to the city - and that taking them might be taking a piece of that magic.

· · ·

This duality is reflected in the many myths and legends that have grown up around the fountain. Some say that if you drink from the Trevi Fountain, you're guaranteed to return to Rome. Others claim that couples who drink together will stay together forever. There are even those who believe that the fountain has the power to grant wishes beyond a mere return to the city.

These beliefs have led to some unusual incidents over the years. In 2007, a man stripped naked and swam in the fountain, claiming he was looking for coins to fund his wedding. In 2016, fashion house Fendi, which had funded a restoration of the fountain, held a fashion show on a plexiglass runway built over the water - much to the consternation of traditionalists who felt it disrespected the fountain's spiritual significance.

But perhaps the most intriguing aspect of the Trevi Fountain's coin tradition is how it has spread beyond Rome. Fountains around the world, from Las Vegas to Tokyo, now feature signs encouraging visitors to toss in coins and make a wish. It's as if a piece of Rome's magic has been exported, a small ritual that connects people across continents.

· · ·

The phenomenon raises interesting questions about the nature of tradition and belief in the modern world. In an age of science and reason, why do so many people still participate in what is essentially a superstitious act? What does it say about our need for ritual, for a connection to something greater than ourselves?

Some anthropologists suggest that the act of throwing a coin into the Trevi Fountain serves as a kind of secular prayer. It's a way for people to externalize their hopes and dreams, to give physical form to their desires. The fountain, with its grand mythological figures and rushing water, becomes a stand-in for the divine - a place where the ordinary can brush up against the extraordinary.

Others see the tradition as a reflection of our relationship with money and value. By throwing away coins - literal currency - we're symbolically prioritizing our wishes over material wealth. It's a small act of faith, a declaration that some things are worth more than money.

But the reality of what happens to the coins adds another layer to this interpretation. The fact that the money goes to charity means that each wish tossed into the fountain has the potential to make a real difference in someone's life. It's a beautiful symmetry - the hopes of visitors helping to fulfill the needs of the city's residents.

Of course, not everyone who tosses a coin into the Trevi Fountain is thinking about charity or anthropological symbolism. For many, it's simply a fun tradition, a must-do item on the Rome tourist checklist. But even in its simplest form, the act connects the individual to the millions who have stood in that spot before, coin in hand, facing away from the rushing water.

The sheer volume of coins tossed into the fountain each year has led to some practical challenges. The weight of all that metal can damage the fountain's structure, requiring regular maintenance. There's also the issue of corrosion - all those coins slowly dissolving in the water can lead to discoloration of the marble.

To combat these issues, the city has implemented various measures over the years. Special coatings have been applied to the fountain's surface to protect it from coin damage. The nightly collection process has been refined to ensure that no coins are left to corrode overnight. There have even been discussions about replacing the water with a non-corrosive liquid, though traditionalists have so far managed to prevent this change.

Despite these challenges, the tradition shows no signs of slowing down. If anything, it seems to be growing stronger. In recent years, there have been reports of people throwing everything from credit cards to cell phones into the fountain, as if upping the ante might increase their chances of a wish coming true.

The Trevi Fountain's coin tradition is a testament to the enduring power of ritual and belief. In a city filled with ancient wonders and historical marvels, this relatively young custom has managed to capture the imagination of millions. It's a reminder that even in our modern, fast-paced world, there's still room for a little magic.

As night falls over Rome and the last coins of the day plunk into the Trevi's waters, one can't help but wonder about the cumulative weight of all those wishes. How many dreams of return have been realized? How many romances sparked? How many lives changed by the simple act of tossing a coin over one's shoulder?

· · ·

The answers to these questions are as elusive as the shimmer of coins beneath the fountain's surface. But as long as people continue to visit Rome, to stand before the grand facade of the Trevi Fountain with hope in their hearts and coins in their hands, the magic will continue. And who knows? Maybe, just maybe, some of those wishes will come true.

22

SANTA MARIA MAGGIORE'S FROZEN FOUNDATION

August in Rome is relentless. The sun beats down on ancient stones, the air shimmers with heat, and even the Tiber seems to flow more sluggishly. It's a time when the city slows down, when Romans who can afford to flee to cooler climes, leaving the streets to hardy tourists and those with no choice but to endure the sweltering days.

But on one August night in 358 AD, something impossible happened. As the city slept, seeking relief from the heat, snow began to fall.

This was no light dusting, no freak weather anomaly quickly melted and forgotten. The snow fell thick and fast, blanketing a section of the Esquiline Hill in a sheet of white. By morning, as stunned Romans emerged from their homes, they found a perfect outline etched in snow - the foundation of what would become one of the city's greatest churches.

This is the story of the Miracle of the Snow, the legendary origin of the Basilica di Santa Maria Maggiore. It's a tale that blends divine intervention with human faith, a moment when the impossible became possible and forever changed the landscape of Rome.

To understand the significance of this miraculous snowfall, we need to step back and look at the Rome of the 4th century. This was a city in transition, caught between its pagan past and its Christian future. The Emperor Constantine had legalized Christianity just a few decades earlier, and the new faith was spreading rapidly. But old beliefs died hard, and many Romans still clung to their traditional gods.

Into this world of changing faiths and shifting allegiances came a wealthy Roman patrician named John and his wife. They were devout Christians, childless and advancing in years. With no heir to inherit their fortune, they decided to dedicate their wealth to the Virgin Mary. But how best to honor her?

As the story goes, John and his wife prayed fervently for guidance. On the night of August 4th, the Virgin Mary appeared to them in a dream. She told them to build a church in her honor on the spot where they would find snow the next morning.

The same night, Pope Liberius had a similar dream. He, too, was instructed to look for a miraculous snowfall that would guide the construction of a new church.

When dawn broke on August 5th, Rome awoke to an astonishing sight. There, on the summit of the Esquiline Hill, lay a patch of fresh snow in the perfect outline of a basilica. News spread quickly through the city. Crowds gathered to see the marvel for themselves, their bare feet sinking into cool white powder under the blazing summer sun.

Pope Liberius, accompanied by John and a growing throng of amazed citizens, made his way to the Esquiline. There, with the miraculous snow as his guide, he began to trace the outline of the future church. Legend has it that as he walked, the snow melted behind him, leaving a clear plan for the builders to follow.

Work on the new basilica began immediately. John and his wife provided the funds, the people of Rome provided the labor, and within a year, the Church of Santa Maria della Neve - Saint Mary of the Snow - stood complete.

Over the centuries, the church would be expanded, embellished, and renamed. Today, it's known as Santa Maria Maggiore - Saint Mary Major - and stands as one of Rome's four great papal basilicas. Its soaring nave, glittering mosaics, and priceless artworks draw visitors from around the world. But at its heart, it remains the church born of a summer snowfall.

The Miracle of the Snow is more than just a quaint legend. It's a story that has shaped the cultural and spiritual life of Rome for nearly two millennia. Each year on August 5th, the feast of the Dedication of Saint Mary Major is celebrated. During the ceremony, a shower of white rose petals is released from the ceiling of the basilica, recreating the miraculous snowfall.

· · ·

This tradition, known as the "miracle of the snow," draws thousands of visitors. As the delicate petals drift down from above, it's easy to imagine that summer night so long ago, when snow fell on Rome and a church was born.

But the influence of the Miracle of the Snow extends far beyond the walls of Santa Maria Maggiore. The story has inspired countless works of art over the centuries. Renaissance masters like Masolino da Panicale created elaborate frescoes depicting the miraculous event. In these paintings, we see Pope Liberius tracing the church's outline in the snow, surrounded by awestruck onlookers.

The miracle has also left its mark on Rome's urban landscape. The area around Santa Maria Maggiore became known as "ad Nives" - "at the Snows" - a name that persisted well into the Middle Ages. Even today, a local gelato shop offers a "Miracle of the Snow" flavor each August, a cool and creamy homage to the basilica's frozen origins.

The story of the miraculous snowfall has traveled far beyond Rome. Churches dedicated to Our Lady of the

Snows can be found around the world, from a tiny chapel in the Philippines to a grand basilica in Missouri. Each of these churches traces its spiritual lineage back to that August night in Rome, when snow fell in summer and a dream became reality.

Of course, not everyone accepts the Miracle of the Snow as historical fact. Skeptics point out that August snowfall in Rome is meteorologically impossible. They suggest that the story was likely invented centuries later to add a divine sheen to the basilica's origins.

These critics note that the first written account of the miracle doesn't appear until the 13th century, nearly 900 years after the supposed event. They argue that the tale was probably created to explain the basilica's unusual orientation - it faces northwest instead of the traditional east - and to cement its status as a major pilgrimage site.

But for many, the literal truth of the story is less important than its spiritual and cultural significance. The Miracle of the Snow speaks to deep human desires - for divine guidance, for clear signs in a confusing world, for the possibility of the impossible. Whether it happened exactly as the legend describes is perhaps less important than what it has meant to countless generations of believers.

The story also reflects the complex religious landscape of 4th century Rome. This was a time when Christianity was ascendant but not yet dominant, when old gods and new faith coexisted in an uneasy balance. The miraculous snowfall can be seen as a kind of divine marketing campaign, a spectacular event designed to win hearts and minds for the new religion.

Indeed, the location of Santa Maria Maggiore is significant. The Esquiline Hill had long been associated with pagan worship, particularly of the goddess Cybele. By building a Christian church on this site, and attaching to it a story of miraculous intervention, the early Church was quite literally claiming ground from the old religion.

This process of building Christian sites on pagan ground was common in Rome and throughout the Empire. It served both practical and symbolic purposes - repurposing existing sacred spaces while also demonstrating the power of the new faith to overcome the old.

.   .   .

The Miracle of the Snow, then, can be seen as part of this larger pattern of religious transformation. It's a story that bridges the gap between pagan Rome and Christian Rome, using elements familiar from older religions - divine visions, miraculous signs - to establish the legitimacy of the new.

But perhaps the most enduring aspect of the Miracle of the Snow is its message of hope and possibility. In a world that often seems random and cruel, the idea that the divine might reach down and leave a clear sign - even one as improbable as snow in August - is deeply appealing. It suggests that we are not alone, that our prayers might be answered in unexpected and wondrous ways.

This message continues to resonate today. Visitors to Santa Maria Maggiore come for many reasons - to admire its art and architecture, to pray, to connect with history. But many also come because of the miracle, drawn by the story of a summer snowfall and a dream made manifest.

As you stand in the basilica's vast nave, gazing up at the coffered ceiling with its gold from the Americas, it's easy to feel overwhelmed by the weight of history and tradition. But then you might notice a detail - a carved snowflake, a wintery motif in a mosaic - and suddenly, you're connected to that long-ago August night.

You can almost feel the cool shock of snow under your feet, see the white flakes drifting down under impossible stars. For a moment, the centuries fall away, and you're there at the beginning, watching a church rise from a field of snow under the height of summer.

This is the lasting power of the Miracle of the Snow. It's a reminder that the extraordinary can break into the ordinary at any moment, that divine providence might be waiting just around the corner. In a city as old as Rome, where every stone seems to tell a story, the tale of Santa Maria Maggiore's snowy foundation still has the power to inspire wonder.

As August's heat shimmers over the city and tourists fan themselves in long queues, the cool interior of Santa Maria Maggiore offers more than just physical relief. It offers a space where miracles feel possible, where summer snow might fall again at any moment. And in that possibility lies the true magic of Rome - a city where the ancient and the eternal meet, where every day might bring a new miracle.

23

THE CURSE OF THE PAPAL TIARA

The Papal Tiara, a towering three-tiered crown, gleams in the soft light of the Vatican Museums. Adorned with precious gems and intricate goldwork, it's a testament to the power and prestige of the papacy. But behind its dazzling facade lies a darker tale - a whispered legend of a curse that has haunted the Holy See for centuries.

They say that to wear the Papal Tiara is to invite tragedy. That those who don this symbol of supreme spiritual authority are marked for an untimely end. It's a superstition that has persisted through the ages, passed down in hushed tones through the corridors of the Vatican and beyond.

. . .

The origins of this curse are as shrouded in mystery as the early history of the tiara itself. Some trace it back to the very beginnings of the papacy, claiming that the weight of such power is inherently dangerous. Others point to specific incidents throughout history, moments when the tiara seemed to bring misfortune to its wearers.

To understand the power of this legend, we must first understand the significance of the Papal Tiara. Unlike a king's crown, which symbolizes earthly authority, the tiara represents something far greater - the Pope's role as the Vicar of Christ, the supreme pontiff of the Catholic Church. Its three tiers are said to represent the Pope's three powers: Father of Kings, Governor of the World, and Vicar of Christ.

The use of the tiara in papal ceremonies dates back to at least the 8th century, though its exact origins are lost to time. Over the centuries, it evolved from a simple cone-shaped cap to an elaborate crown, each pope adding his own touches and embellishments. By the Renaissance, the tiara had become a work of art in its own right, encrusted with jewels and crafted from the finest materials.

. . .

But with this increasing grandeur came increasing danger - or so the legends say. Tales began to circulate of popes who met with misfortune shortly after their coronation, their reigns cut short by illness, assassination, or mysterious circumstances.

One of the earliest examples often cited in connection with the curse is Pope Celestine V. Elected in 1294, Celestine was a humble hermit who was reluctant to accept the papal throne. After just five months, overwhelmed by the burdens of office, he became the first pope in history to resign voluntarily. He died less than two years later, possibly murdered on the orders of his successor.

Then there's the tragic tale of Pope Urban VI, crowned in 1378. His reign was marked by extreme cruelty and paranoia, leading some to speculate that the weight of the tiara had unbalanced his mind. He died in 1389, possibly poisoned by his own cardinals who could no longer tolerate his erratic behavior.

The list goes on through the centuries. Pope Pius III, who wore the tiara for just 26 days before succumbing to an infection. Pope Leo XI, whose reign lasted a mere 27 days before he too passed away. Pope John Paul I, the "Smiling

Pope," who died suddenly after only 33 days in office, sparking countless conspiracy theories.

Of course, skeptics are quick to point out that correlation does not imply causation. The papacy, particularly in earlier centuries, was a dangerous office regardless of headwear. Popes faced threats from rival claimants, hostile secular rulers, and even their own cardinals. Many were elderly when elected, making short reigns and sudden deaths not uncommon.

Yet the legend persists, fueled by the human tendency to see patterns in random events and our fascination with the idea of power coming at a terrible price. The curse of the Papal Tiara taps into something primal - the fear that reaching for greatness might invite divine retribution.

This superstition has had real-world consequences. Some popes, wary of the curse, chose to delay their coronation or modify the ceremony. Pope John Paul I, aware of the whispers surrounding the tiara, opted for a simpler inauguration without the traditional crowning. His successor, John Paul II, went even further, permanently abandoning the use of the tiara in papal ceremonies.

. . .

The last pope to be crowned with the tiara was Paul VI in 1963. In a symbolic gesture at the end of the Second Vatican Council in 1965, he descended from his throne, removed his tiara, and placed it on the altar of St. Peter's Basilica. It was his way of emphasizing the servant nature of the papacy and distancing the Church from the trappings of worldly power.

Yet even this act of humility couldn't entirely shake off the tiara's sinister reputation. Some saw Paul VI's gesture not just as a symbol of papal humility, but as an attempt to break the curse once and for all. By giving up the tiara voluntarily, perhaps he hoped to lift the shadow that had hung over the papacy for so long.

The power of the curse lies not just in its supposed effects on the popes who wore the tiara, but in what it represents. It's a reminder that even the highest spiritual authority on Earth is not immune to human frailty and mortality. The tiara, with its triple crown and glittering jewels, may symbolize divine authority, but the men who wear it remain all too human.

. . .

This duality - the tension between the divine office and the mortal officeholder - has been a central theme in the history of the papacy. The curse of the tiara can be seen as a metaphor for this struggle, a cautionary tale about the dangers of conflating earthly power with spiritual authority.

In many ways, the legend of the cursed tiara reflects broader cultural attitudes towards power and its corrupting influence. It's a theme that runs through countless stories and myths across cultures - the idea that great power comes at a great price. From the Ring of Gyges in Plato's Republic to the One Ring in Tolkien's Lord of the Rings, we see this concept played out again and again.

The curse also speaks to our fascination with the inner workings of one of the world's oldest and most secretive institutions. The Vatican, with its centuries of history and hidden archives, has long been a source of mystery and intrigue. The idea of a cursed crown at the heart of this institution adds another layer to its mystique.

In recent years, the legend of the cursed tiara has found new life in popular culture. It's been featured in novels,

TV shows, and conspiracy theories. Each new iteration adds to the myth, embellishing the tale and ensuring its survival in the public imagination.

But what of the tiara itself? Today, the Papal Tiara is no longer used in official ceremonies. The last few popes have opted for a simpler mitre, emphasizing their role as bishops of Rome rather than temporal rulers. The tiaras of past popes are now museum pieces, objects of historical and artistic interest rather than symbols of current papal authority.

Yet even as museum exhibits, they continue to fascinate. Visitors to the Vatican Museums often pause before the display of papal tiaras, drawn in by their beauty and the weight of history they represent. And perhaps, in the back of their minds, they remember the whispered tales of the curse.

The Papal Tiara serves as a potent symbol of the complexities and contradictions inherent in the papacy. It represents supreme spiritual authority, yet its ornate design speaks to worldly wealth and power. It's a crown, yet it adorns the head of a man who is supposed to be a servant of servants. And hanging over it all is the shadow of the curse, a reminder of the precarious nature of power and the inevitability of mortality.

As we look at the tiara today, safely ensconced behind museum glass, it's easy to dismiss the idea of a curse as mere superstition. But in doing so, we perhaps miss the deeper truth that this legend points to. The real curse of the Papal Tiara isn't some supernatural hex, but the very human challenges that come with wielding great power and responsibility.

Every pope who has worn the tiara has had to grapple with these challenges. How to balance spiritual leadership with worldly concerns? How to wield authority without being corrupted by it? How to bear the weight of centuries of tradition while adapting to a changing world? These are the real burdens of the papal office, far heavier than any jewel-encrusted crown.

In this light, the abandonment of the tiara in modern papal ceremonies can be seen not just as a break with tradition, but as an acknowledgment of these deeper truths. By setting aside the crown, modern popes are perhaps attempting to focus on the essence of their role, stripped of its medieval trappings.

. . .

Yet the legend of the curse endures, a testament to our enduring fascination with power, spirituality, and the thin line between them. It reminds us that even in our modern, rationalistic world, there's still room for mystery and superstition. And it challenges us to consider the true nature of leadership and the prices we pay for power.

The next time you find yourself in the Vatican Museums, standing before the glittering Papal Tiara, take a moment to reflect. Behind its dazzling exterior lies a story of power and peril, of curses and challenges, of human frailty and divine authority. It's a crown that has shaped history, inspired legends, and continues to captivate us to this day. And who knows? Perhaps, just perhaps, there's more to the curse than mere superstition after all.

24

LOCUSTA: ROME'S EMPRESS OF POISON

In the annals of Roman history, few figures are as sinister and intriguing as Locusta. Her name, whispered in fear through the marble halls of palaces and the grimy back alleys of ancient Rome, was synonymous with a particularly insidious form of death: poison. Locusta was not just a murderer; she was an artist, a master of toxic concoctions who turned assassination into a refined craft.

The exact origins of Locusta are shrouded in mystery. Some accounts claim she hailed from Gaul, bringing with her the secret knowledge of herbs and potions from the druidic traditions. Others suggest she was a local Roman, born into the underworld of the eternal city and schooled in the dark arts from a young age. Whatever her beginnings, by the time she rose to infamy in the imperial court, Locusta had honed her skills to deadly perfection.

Locusta's rise to prominence coincided with one of the most turbulent periods in Roman history. The Julio-Claudian dynasty, founded by the great Augustus, was in its twilight years. Emperors rose and fell with alarming frequency, often meeting violent ends. In this atmosphere of constant intrigue and backstabbing, Locusta's particular talents were in high demand.

Her first significant appearance in the historical record comes during the reign of Claudius, the stammering emperor who had unexpectedly come to power after the assassination of his nephew, Caligula. Claudius, despite his physical infirmities, had proven to be a capable ruler. But as he aged, the question of succession loomed large over the imperial court.

Claudius had a son, Britannicus, who was his natural heir. But he also had an adopted son, Nero, the child of his fourth wife, Agrippina the Younger. Agrippina, a woman of boundless ambition, was determined to see her son on the throne, even if it meant removing Claudius from the picture.

. . .

It was in this web of familial intrigue that Locusta found her opportunity. Agrippina, seeking a way to eliminate Claudius without arousing suspicion, turned to the notorious poisoner. Locusta was tasked with creating a poison that would mimic the effects of illness, allowing Agrippina to remove her husband while maintaining the appearance of a natural death.

The poison Locusta concocted was a masterpiece of toxic engineering. According to historical accounts, it was delivered to Claudius in a dish of mushrooms, his favorite delicacy. The emperor consumed the tainted fungi and soon fell ill. However, whether due to his robust constitution or an miscalculation in the dosage, Claudius did not immediately succumb.

Panic gripped Agrippina and her conspirators. They could not risk Claudius recovering and potentially discovering their plot. In desperation, they called upon Locusta once again. This time, she provided a more potent poison, which was allegedly administered to the emperor via a feather used to induce vomiting - a common practice in Roman medicine. This second dose proved fatal, and Claudius breathed his last in October of 54 AD.

. . .

With Claudius dead, Nero ascended to the throne. But Locusta's services were far from over. The young emperor, guided by his mother's machinations, soon found himself in need of the poisoner's skills once again.

Britannicus, Claudius's biological son, remained a threat to Nero's rule. Though young, he was approaching manhood and could potentially challenge Nero's claim to the throne. The solution, in Nero's mind, was clear: Britannicus had to be eliminated.

Once again, Locusta was called upon to ply her deadly trade. This time, the challenge was even greater. Britannicus, aware of the danger he was in, had taken to employing food tasters to check his meals for poison. Locusta needed to create a toxin that would evade detection but still prove swiftly fatal.

Her solution was ingenious and horrifying in equal measure. She developed a poison that was inert when cold but became deadly when heated. The toxic substance was slipped into Britannicus's drink. When hot water was added to dilute the wine, as was the Roman custom, the poison activated.

The effects were immediate and dramatic. Britannicus collapsed at the dinner table, his body wracked with convulsions. Nero, displaying a callousness that would come to characterize his reign, dismissed the incident as an epileptic fit - a condition Britannicus had suffered from in childhood. By the time the ruse became clear, Britannicus was dead, and Nero's position was secure.

For her services, Locusta was richly rewarded. Nero granted her a pardon for her past crimes, gifted her with extensive estates, and even set up a school where she could teach her craft to others. Under imperial patronage, Locusta's poisoning academy flourished, producing a new generation of toxic assassins.

But the poisoner's favored status was not to last. As Nero's reign descended into tyranny and madness, Locusta found herself increasingly involved in the emperor's paranoid schemes. She was called upon to create poisons for numerous victims, real and imagined, as Nero sought to eliminate anyone he perceived as a threat.

· · ·

Locusta's fate was tied inextricably to that of her imperial patron. When Nero's rule finally collapsed in 68 AD, leading to his suicide, Locusta found herself suddenly vulnerable. The protection she had enjoyed under Nero vanished overnight, and all the enemies she had made over the years saw their chance for revenge.

The new emperor, Galba, was quick to act against those associated with Nero's regime. Locusta was arrested and paraded through the streets of Rome in chains, a spectacle for the masses who both feared and reviled her. Her execution was public and deliberately humiliating, designed to serve as a warning to others who might follow in her footsteps.

Yet even in death, Locusta's legacy lived on. The secrets of her poisons, passed down through her school, continued to circulate in Rome's underworld. For years after her execution, whenever a mysterious death occurred in the upper echelons of Roman society, whispers of Locusta's name could be heard.

The story of Locusta is more than just a tale of a skilled poisoner. It's a window into the dark underbelly of imperial Rome, a world where power was fleeting and death could come at any moment, from any direction. In this environment, someone with Locusta's talents could rise from obscurity to become a key player in the highest levels of Roman politics.

Locusta's life and crimes also raise intriguing questions about the nature of power and morality in ancient Rome. Was she merely a tool, wielded by those in power to achieve their ends? Or was she an active participant, using her skills to manipulate the great game of Roman politics for her own benefit?

The answer, perhaps, lies somewhere in between. Locusta was undoubtedly a willing participant in numerous murders, but she was also a product of her time. In a society where violence and treachery were commonplace, particularly in the imperial court, her skills offered a path to wealth and influence that would have been otherwise closed to her.

Moreover, Locusta's story highlights the complex relationship between science, medicine, and crime in the ancient world. Her knowledge of herbs and poisons likely drew from the same well as that of healers and physicians. The line between medicine and poison, between healing and harm, was often blurry in ancient Rome.

In many ways, Locusta represents a dark reflection of the knowledge and power that Rome had accumulated as the center of a vast empire. The same trade networks that brought spices and silks from the far corners of the known world also provided access to exotic and deadly substances. The multicultural nature of the empire meant that traditional knowledge from various regions could be combined in new and potentially lethal ways.

The legacy of Locusta extends far beyond her own time. Her name became a byword for poisoners in later centuries, and her techniques were studied and emulated by assassins for generations. The fear she instilled in the Roman elite led to increased paranoia about poisoning, influencing everything from dinner etiquette to the design of drinking vessels.

Even today, the name of Locusta continues to fascinate. She appears in novels, plays, and historical documentaries, a symbol of the darker side of Roman power and the eternal human fascination with the art of murder. Her story serves as a reminder that behind the grand monuments and noble ideals of ancient Rome lay a world of intrigue, betrayal, and silent, invisible death.

As you walk the streets of modern Rome, surrounded by the remnants of its imperial past, spare a thought for Locusta. In the shadows of grand palaces and majestic temples, you might just catch an echo of her enduring influence - a reminder that even in the eternal city, nothing lasts forever, and death can come in the most unexpected forms.

25

CARAVAGGIO: THE FUGITIVE ARTIST

Rome, 1606. The eternal city pulsed with life, its streets a canvas of light and shadow. In a dimly lit tavern, a game of tennis was about to change the course of art history. Michelangelo Merisi da Caravaggio, the enfant terrible of Roman painting, faced off against Ranuccio Tomassoni, a man whose name would be forever linked to the artist's downfall.

The exact details of what happened that night remain shrouded in mystery. Some say it was a dispute over a bet, others a quarrel over a woman. Whatever the cause, the confrontation escalated quickly. Swords were drawn, and in the chaos that followed, Tomassoni fell, mortally wounded. Caravaggio, his own blade stained with blood, fled into the night.

· · ·

This moment marked the beginning of Caravaggio's life as a fugitive. The brash young painter who had taken Rome by storm, shocking and delighting patrons with his revolutionary use of light and unflinching realism, was now a wanted man. The Pope issued a bando capitale, a death warrant that allowed anyone to kill Caravaggio with impunity.

Caravaggio's flight from Rome was the start of a four-year odyssey that would take him across Italy and beyond, always one step ahead of the law, always seeking redemption through his art. His first stop was the estate of his patrons, the powerful Colonna family. They sheltered him briefly before arranging his escape to Naples, then under Spanish rule and beyond the Pope's jurisdiction.

In Naples, Caravaggio found a city as dramatic and volatile as his own temperament. His reputation as an artist had preceded him, and commissions soon followed. The Neapolitan period saw the creation of some of his most powerful works, including "The Seven Works of Mercy" and "The Flagellation of Christ." These paintings, with their stark contrasts and emotional intensity, reflected the turmoil of the artist's life.

.   .   .

But Naples was not far enough. Caravaggio's paranoia, fueled by real threats to his life, drove him further south. He set sail for Malta, the island stronghold of the Knights of St. John. Here, he hoped to earn a knighthood, a title that would grant him immunity from prosecution.

On Malta, Caravaggio's fortunes seemed to turn. His paintings impressed the Grand Master of the Knights, and he was inducted into the order. His masterpiece from this period, "The Beheading of Saint John the Baptist," still hangs in the Co-Cathedral of St. John in Valletta. It's the only work he ever signed, painting his name in the blood flowing from the saint's severed neck - a grim reminder of his own violent past.

But Caravaggio's temper and penchant for trouble followed him even to this island sanctuary. Within months of his knighthood, he was involved in another brawl. This time, his opponent was a fellow knight. Caravaggio found himself imprisoned in the formidable Fort Sant'Angelo. It seemed his luck had finally run out.

.   .   .

Yet, in a twist worthy of one of his dramatic canvases, Caravaggio managed to escape. How he broke out of one of the most secure fortresses in the Mediterranean remains a mystery. Some suggest he had help from high-placed friends, others that he used his artistic skills to forge documents. Whatever the method, Caravaggio was once again on the run.

He fled to Sicily, moving from city to city, always looking over his shoulder. His time on the island produced works of haunting power, like "The Burial of Saint Lucy" in Syracuse and "The Raising of Lazarus" in Messina. These paintings show a marked shift in style - gone are the vibrant colors and sensual figures of his Roman period. In their place are somber tones and faces marked by despair and resignation.

Caravaggio's brush seemed to channel his inner turmoil. His figures, always known for their stark realism, now took on an almost ghostly quality. The artist who had once painted himself as a cocky young Bacchus now portrayed himself as the severed head of Goliath, his face a mask of pain and regret.

· · ·

But Sicily was not the end of Caravaggio's journey. Reports that he had been pardoned by the Pope led him to set sail for Rome in 1610. It was a fateful decision. The circumstances of his final days are as mysterious as much of his life. Some accounts say he was arrested in a case of mistaken identity upon landing in Palo. Others suggest he died of a fever on the beach at Port'Ercole.

What's certain is that Caravaggio never made it back to Rome. The man who had revolutionized painting, who had brought a gritty realism and dramatic use of light to religious art, died far from the city that had made him famous. He was just 38 years old.

In death, as in life, Caravaggio remained a figure of controversy. For centuries, his work fell out of favor, dismissed as too dark, too realistic, too much a reflection of his troubled life. It wasn't until the 20th century that his genius was fully recognized, his influence on Western art finally acknowledged.

Today, Caravaggio is celebrated as one of the greatest painters of all time. His works command audiences wherever they're displayed, their power undimmed by the passage of four centuries. But perhaps even more compelling than his art is the story of the man himself - the fugitive artist whose life was as dramatic as any of his canvases.

Caravaggio's years on the run were more than just a flight from justice. They were a journey into the depths of his own psyche, a constant battle between his genius and his demons. Each city he visited, each painting he created, added another layer to the complex portrait of the artist.

In Naples, we see Caravaggio at his most prolific, churning out masterpieces even as he looked over his shoulder for assassins. His "Madonna of the Rosary" from this period shows the Virgin Mary turning away from the viewer, as if sharing in the artist's need to hide.

On Malta, Caravaggio reached the heights of recognition, only to fall spectacularly. His "Saint Jerome Writing," painted during his brief time as a Knight, shows the saint hunched over his work, his face a study in concentration and inner torment - perhaps a reflection of the artist's own state of mind.

· · ·

In Sicily, we find a Caravaggio stripped of his bravado, facing his own mortality. His "Adoration of the Shepherds" in Messina is a study in humility, the figures gathered around the Christ child seeming to emerge from darkness into light - a metaphor, perhaps, for the redemption the artist sought.

Through it all, Caravaggio's art continued to evolve. The theatrical lighting that had made him famous in Rome became more pronounced, the contrasts between light and dark more extreme. His figures, always startlingly real, now seemed to carry the weight of the world on their shoulders.

But it wasn't just his painting style that changed during these fugitive years. Caravaggio's choice of subjects shifted as well. Gone were the seductive young men and women of his early career. In their place were saints and martyrs, figures grappling with faith and facing death. It's tempting to see in these choices a reflection of Caravaggio's own struggles, his attempt to come to terms with his actions and his fate.

The story of Caravaggio's final years is more than just a tale of an artist on the run. It's a story about the relationship between art and life, about the ways in which personal experience shapes creative expression. In Caravaggio's case, his fugitive status seemed to drive him to even greater artistic heights, as if he were racing against time to leave his mark on the world.

It's also a story about the price of genius. Caravaggio's talent was undeniable, but it came coupled with a volatile temperament and a disregard for social norms that repeatedly landed him in trouble. His life raises questions about the nature of artistic temperament and the sometimes fine line between brilliance and madness.

In the end, Caravaggio's legacy is as complex as the man himself. He left behind a body of work that continues to captivate and inspire, paintings that seem to pulse with life even centuries after their creation. But he also left behind a trail of violence and controversy, a life story that reads like a Renaissance crime novel.

Perhaps that's why Caravaggio continues to fascinate us today. In his art and in his life, we see the full spectrum of human experience - the sublime and the sordid, the divine and the all too human. His fugitive years, in particular, speak to something universal: the struggle for redemption, the quest to outrun one's past, the hope that through our work, we might transcend our flaws and leave something lasting behind.

As we stand before a Caravaggio painting today, whether in Rome or Naples, Malta or Sicily, we're not just looking at a masterpiece of technique and composition. We're looking at a snapshot of a life lived on the edge, a testament to the power of art to emerge from even the darkest of circumstances. In those dramatic plays of light and shadow, we can still feel the presence of the fugitive artist, forever running, forever seeking, forever painting his way towards immortality.

26

STARGAZER ON TRIAL: THE INQUISITION OF GALILEO GALILEI

The year was 1633, and Rome was abuzz with whispers and speculation. In the halls of power and on the cobblestone streets, one name was on everyone's lips: Galileo Galilei. The renowned astronomer and physicist, once celebrated in the papal courts, now found himself at the center of a storm that would shake the foundations of science and faith.

Galileo's journey to this pivotal moment had been long and winding. Born in Pisa in 1564, he had shown an early aptitude for mathematics and natural philosophy. His inquiring mind and innovative experiments had earned him fame across Europe. He improved the telescope, made groundbreaking observations of the heavens, and championed a new way of understanding the universe.

· · ·

But it was this new understanding that had brought him into conflict with the Catholic Church. Galileo supported the heliocentric model of the solar system, which placed the Sun at the center with the Earth and other planets orbiting around it. This view, first proposed by Copernicus nearly a century earlier, contradicted the geocentric model that had been accepted for millennia and was supported by church doctrine.

The conflict between Galileo and the Church had been brewing for years. In 1616, the Inquisition had declared heliocentrism to be heretical. Galileo was ordered to abandon his support for the theory. For a time, he complied, at least outwardly. But his mind continued to work, his observations continued to challenge the old models, and eventually, he could no longer stay silent.

In 1632, Galileo published his "Dialogue Concerning the Two Chief World Systems." Although presented as a balanced debate between the Copernican and Ptolemaic systems, it was clear to most readers that Galileo favored the heliocentric model. The book was an immediate sensation, but it also sealed Galileo's fate. The Inquisition summoned him to Rome to stand trial for heresy.

· · ·

As Galileo made his way to Rome in the early months of 1633, the city was a hotbed of intrigue. The Thirty Years' War was raging across Europe, and the Church was fighting its own battles against the rising tide of Protestantism. In this climate of fear and suspicion, Galileo's ideas were seen not just as scientific theories, but as dangerous challenges to the Church's authority.

The trial began in April. Galileo, now nearly 70 years old and in failing health, faced the stern judges of the Inquisition. The proceedings were held in the Palace of the Inquisition, a forbidding building that struck fear into the hearts of those summoned before it. Here, in rooms where others had been tortured and condemned, Galileo would have to defend not just his ideas, but his very life.

The charges against Galileo were serious. He was accused of heresy, of disobeying the Church's previous injunction against teaching heliocentrism, and of misleading the censors who had approved his book. The prosecution presented letters and testimony suggesting that Galileo had been explicitly forbidden from promoting Copernican ideas in any way.

·　·　·

Galileo's defense was careful and strategic. He argued that his book did not definitively promote heliocentrism, but merely presented it as a hypothesis. He claimed that he had not remembered the specific injunctions against teaching the theory. He presented character witnesses who attested to his piety and obedience to the Church.

But the outcome of the trial seemed predetermined. The Inquisition was not interested in debating the merits of Galileo's scientific observations. Their concern was with obedience to Church doctrine and authority. In their eyes, Galileo had defied a direct order and challenged the Church's position on a fundamental question of how the universe was ordered.

After weeks of questioning and deliberation, the verdict was announced. Galileo was found "vehemently suspect of heresy." He was forced to recant his support for heliocentrism, denouncing his life's work in a public ceremony. Legend has it that after his recantation, Galileo muttered under his breath, "And yet it moves," referring to the Earth's orbit around the Sun. While this dramatic moment likely never happened, it captures the spirit of a man forced to deny what he knew to be true.

. . .

The sentence was harsh, but not as severe as it could have been. Galileo was placed under house arrest for the remainder of his life. His "Dialogue" was banned, and he was forbidden from publishing any new works. The man who had once been feted in Rome's grandest palaces would spend his final years as a prisoner in his own home.

The impact of Galileo's trial reverberated far beyond Rome. It sent a chill through the scientific community, warning other researchers to be cautious in challenging established doctrines. For centuries afterward, the trial would be held up as a prime example of the conflict between science and religion.

But the story of Galileo's trial is more complex than a simple battle between reason and faith. It was also a political struggle, caught up in the power dynamics of 17th century Europe. The Catholic Church, feeling threatened by the Protestant Reformation and new scientific ideas, was asserting its authority wherever it could.

Moreover, Galileo's own actions had contributed to his downfall. His abrasive personality and his tendency to mock his opponents had made him enemies in powerful places. His insistence on publishing his ideas in Italian, rather than the scholarly Latin, made his work accessible to a wider audience - and thus more threatening to the established order.

Despite the Church's efforts, Galileo's ideas could not be suppressed forever. Copies of his banned books were smuggled across Europe, inspiring a new generation of scientists and philosophers. The scientific revolution that Galileo had helped to start continued to gain momentum, gradually reshaping humanity's understanding of the universe.

Galileo himself never gave up on his work, even under house arrest. In his final years, going blind but with his mind still sharp, he dictated his last and perhaps greatest book, "Discourses and Mathematical Demonstrations Relating to Two New Sciences." This work, which laid the foundations for modern physics, was smuggled out of Italy and published in the Netherlands, beyond the reach of the Inquisition.

The legacy of Galileo's trial continues to be debated today. For some, it represents the triumph of dogma over reason, a cautionary tale about the dangers of allowing religious or political ideology to suppress scientific inquiry. For others, it's a more nuanced story about the complex relationship between science and society, and the challenges of navigating a world where new ideas clash with established beliefs.

In 1992, more than 350 years after Galileo's trial, Pope John Paul II issued a formal apology for the Church's treatment of the astronomer. This gesture, while largely symbolic, represented a significant shift in the Church's approach to science. Today, the Vatican even has its own astronomical observatory, continuing the work that Galileo began four centuries ago.

Visitors to Rome can still see reminders of Galileo's story. The Church of Santa Maria sopra Minerva, where Galileo was forced to recant his beliefs, still stands. The nearby Pantheon, with its perfect dome open to the sky, seems an apt monument to a man who spent his life studying the heavens. And in the Vatican Museums, a gold-plated telescope serves as a reminder of the instrument that allowed Galileo to challenge humanity's view of the cosmos.

· · ·

As we look back on the trial of Galileo, we're reminded of the power of ideas to shape the world. Galileo's observations, made with a simple telescope, set in motion a revolution in human thought that continues to this day. His story is a testament to the enduring human drive to understand our place in the universe, even in the face of opposition and persecution.

In the end, Galileo's famous (if apocryphal) mutter - "And yet it moves" - proved prophetic. The Earth does indeed move around the Sun, and our understanding of the cosmos continues to evolve. Galileo's trial may have been a setback for science, but it could not stop the forward march of human knowledge. In the centuries since, we've sent probes to distant planets, peered into the hearts of galaxies, and begun to unravel the mysteries of the universe that Galileo could only dream of exploring.

The tale of Galileo reminds us that the pursuit of truth is rarely easy, but always essential. It challenges us to question our assumptions, to look at the world with fresh eyes, and to have the courage to stand by our convictions, even when they clash with prevailing wisdom. In this way, the spirit of Galileo lives on, not just in the annals of scientific history, but in every person who dares to look up at the stars and ask, "What if?"

27

THE VANISHING SPLENDOR: THE MYSTERY OF DIOCLETIAN'S BATHS

Once, they were a marvel of Rome, a testament to the empire's grandeur and engineering prowess. The Baths of Diocletian stood as a colossal monument to luxury and leisure, a place where citizens could escape the heat and grime of the city to indulge in the rituals of cleansing and socializing. Today, only fragments remain, scattered across the landscape of modern Rome like pieces of a forgotten puzzle. The story of these baths - their rise, their fall, and their mysterious disappearance - is a tale that spans centuries and speaks volumes about the ebb and flow of civilizations.

Construction of the Baths began in 298 AD, during the reign of Emperor Diocletian. The Roman Empire was entering its twilight years, but you wouldn't have known it from the scale of this project. Covering an area of over 13 hectares, the Baths of Diocletian were the largest of their kind in the ancient world. They could accommodate up to 3,000 bathers at a time, a staggering number that gives us a sense of the sheer magnitude of Roman urban life.

The complex was more than just a place to bathe. It was a city within a city, featuring gardens, libraries, galleries, and spaces for exercise and relaxation. The central bathing block alone covered an area of 90,000 square meters. Visitors would progress through a series of rooms, each serving a different purpose in the bathing ritual. There was the frigidarium for cold baths, the tepidarium for warm baths, and the caldarium for hot baths. Steam rooms, massage areas, and spaces for socializing and business dealings completed the experience.

The architecture was as impressive as the scale. Soaring vaulted ceilings, supported by massive granite columns, created a sense of awe and spaciousness. The walls were adorned with fine marbles, intricate mosaics, and elaborate frescoes. Statues of gods, emperors, and heroes stood in niches and courtyards, turning the baths into a veritable outdoor museum.

· · ·

But perhaps the most remarkable aspect of the Baths of Diocletian was the sophisticated engineering that made it all possible. An extensive network of underground chambers and passages housed the complex machinery needed to heat and circulate water throughout the baths. Aqueducts brought water from distant springs, while hypocaust systems - essentially ancient underfloor heating - kept the rooms warm. It was a triumph of Roman ingenuity, a perfect marriage of luxury and technology.

For centuries, the Baths of Diocletian were a central feature of Roman life. They survived the fall of the Western Roman Empire in 476 AD and continued to function, albeit in a reduced capacity, under the Ostrogothic kings who ruled Italy in the following decades. But then, sometime in the 6th century, the baths fell into disuse. The exact reasons for this decline remain a mystery, one of the many enigmas surrounding the fate of this once-great complex.

Some historians speculate that the Gothic Wars, which ravaged Italy in the mid-6th century, may have played a role. The siege of Rome in 537 AD by the Ostrogothic king Vitiges led to the cutting of the aqueducts that supplied water to the city. Without a steady water supply, the baths would have been rendered useless. Others suggest that changing social norms and the rise of Christianity, which sometimes viewed public bathing with suspicion, contributed to the baths' abandonment.

Whatever the cause, the Baths of Diocletian began a long, slow process of decay. As Rome's population dwindled in the early Middle Ages, the massive complex became an easy target for looters and scavengers. Precious marbles were stripped away, bronze fittings were melted down, and even the lead pipes that had once carried water throughout the baths were torn out and repurposed.

But the disappearance of the Baths of Diocletian wasn't just a matter of physical decay. It was as if the very memory of the place began to fade from the collective consciousness of Rome. The once-bustling halls fell silent, the grand chambers were reclaimed by nature, and the intricate machinery that had once heated and circulated water throughout the complex rusted away in forgotten underground chambers.

As the centuries passed, the remnants of the baths took on new roles. Parts of the structure were incorporated into other buildings. The central hall, with its massive vaulted ceiling still intact, was transformed into the Church of

Santa Maria degli Angeli e dei Martiri in the 16th century, under the direction of Michelangelo. Other sections became granaries, storehouses, or were simply left to crumble.

The disappearance of the Baths of Diocletian wasn't just a loss of a building; it was the vanishing of an entire way of life. The baths had been more than just a place to get clean. They were a social hub, a place where people of all classes could mingle, where ideas were exchanged, deals were struck, and the pulse of the city could be felt. Their abandonment marked a profound shift in urban life, a step away from the public, communal culture of ancient Rome towards the more private, fragmented society of medieval Europe.

But perhaps the most intriguing aspect of the Baths of Diocletian's disappearance is the fate of its treasures. The baths had been filled with works of art - statues, mosaics, frescoes - many of which simply vanished. Some, no doubt, were destroyed or repurposed over the centuries. But others may have been hidden away, either by looters hoping to return for them later or by caretakers trying to protect them from destruction.

.   .   .

Rumors and legends have persisted for centuries about hidden chambers beneath the baths, filled with priceless artifacts. Every so often, a new discovery seems to lend credence to these tales. In the 19th century, excavations uncovered a number of fine statues that had somehow escaped the notice of looters. More recently, ground-penetrating radar has revealed the existence of previously unknown underground structures, hinting at the possibility of further discoveries.

The gradual rediscovery of the Baths of Diocletian began in earnest during the Renaissance, as scholars and artists became fascinated with the ruins of ancient Rome. The great architect Andrea Palladio studied and sketched the remains of the baths, using what he learned to influence his own designs. These early studies helped preserve at least some knowledge of the baths' original layout and appearance.

In the 20th century, systematic archaeological excavations began to uncover more of the baths' secrets. Bit by bit, the true scale and sophistication of the complex became apparent. Yet even today, much of the site remains unexplored. The sheer size of the baths, combined with the fact that much of modern Rome is built atop their remains, makes a complete excavation challenging.

. . .

Today, visitors to Rome can still see fragments of the Baths of Diocletian scattered throughout the city. The best-preserved section is the central hall, now the Church of Santa Maria degli Angeli e dei Martiri. Here, standing beneath the soaring 27-meter high vaults, one can get a sense of the awe that ancient Romans must have felt. The National Roman Museum, housed in part of the baths complex, displays artifacts recovered from the site and offers a glimpse into the luxurious lifestyle the baths once provided.

Yet for all that has been discovered, the Baths of Diocletian remain shrouded in mystery. How did such a massive, important complex fall into ruin so completely? What treasures might still lie hidden beneath the streets of modern Rome? And what can the fate of the baths tell us about the fall of Rome and the transition from the ancient to the medieval world?

The story of the Baths of Diocletian is, in many ways, the story of Rome itself. It's a tale of ambition and engineering prowess, of luxury and decay, of loss and rediscovery. As we walk among the remnants of the baths today, we're not just exploring an archaeological site.

We're touching the pulse of history, connecting with the daily lives of people who lived and bathed and socialized here two thousand years ago.

The disappearance of the Baths of Diocletian serves as a poignant reminder of the impermanence of even the grandest human achievements. It challenges us to consider what aspects of our own civilization might one day become mysterious ruins for future generations to puzzle over. And yet, it also speaks to the enduring nature of human curiosity and our drive to understand our past.

As archaeologists continue to uncover new sections of the baths and historians reinterpret the evidence, the full story of the Baths of Diocletian is still being written. Each discovery, each pieced-together fragment, adds another chapter to this epic tale of rise and fall, of splendor and ruin. The baths may have vanished from view for centuries, but they never truly disappeared. They were always there, waiting beneath the streets of Rome, holding their secrets until the time was right to reveal them once more.

28

THE PHANTOM BELLS OF SAN CLEMENTE

The Basilica of San Clemente stands as a testament to Rome's layered history, a physical embodiment of the city's evolution through the ages. But beneath its Romanesque façade and medieval frescoes lies a mystery that has puzzled visitors and locals alike for centuries: the legend of the phantom bells.

On certain nights, when the city sleeps and silence blankets the ancient streets, some claim to hear the faint tolling of bells emanating from the depths of San Clemente. These are not the church's actual bells, which hang silent in the tower above. No, these phantom bells ring from somewhere far below, in the unseen layers of history that lie beneath the basilica.

. . .

To understand the legend of the phantom bells, we must first peel back the layers of San Clemente itself. The current church, dating from the 12th century, is just the topmost layer of a historical cake that descends deep into Rome's past. Beneath it lies a 4th-century basilica, and below that, the remains of a 1st-century Roman house and a 2nd-century Mithraic temple.

This vertical journey through time reflects Rome's complex religious history. The pagan gave way to the Christian, but not without leaving its mark. The Mithraic temple, once a place where followers of the mysterious cult of Mithras gathered in secret, now sits silent and dark beneath the weight of centuries of Christian worship.

It's from this lowest level, some say, that the phantom bells ring. But why? And how? The stories vary, each adding a new layer to the mystery, much like the layers of the basilica itself.

One tale speaks of a pagan priest, the last of his kind, who retreated to the underground temple as Christianity swept through Rome. As the new basilica was built above, sealing him in, he forged a set of bells from the sacred metals of his faith. These bells, the story goes, he rings eternally, a defiant reminder of the old gods in the face of the new.

Another legend tells of early Christian martyrs, imprisoned in the Roman house before it was converted to a church. In their darkest hours, they heard the comforting toll of heavenly bells, promising salvation. Now, it's said, those same bells ring out occasionally, offering hope to those in despair.

A third story, darker than the rest, whispers of a demon trapped by Saint Clement himself when the first church was consecrated. The bells, in this telling, are the creature's attempt to call for release, a haunting reminder of the spiritual battles waged in Rome's early Christian days.

Whatever the source, the phantom bells of San Clemente have captured the imagination of Romans and visitors for generations. They've inspired artists, writers, and musicians, each trying to capture the ethereal quality of those unseen chimes.

But the legend of the bells is more than just a ghost story. It's a metaphor for the way Rome's past continues to echo into its present. The city is built on layers upon layers of history, each new era building upon the ruins of the last. Sometimes, like at San Clemente, this layering is literal. More often, it's figurative, with ancient traditions and beliefs persisting in modified forms through the centuries.

The phantom bells remind us that the past is never truly silent. It speaks to us through ruins and relics, through stories and legends, and sometimes, if we listen closely, through the ghostly toll of long-forgotten bells.

Visitors to San Clemente today can explore its various levels, descending through time as they go. The current basilica, with its glittering mosaics and intricate frescoes, gives way to the starker beauty of the 4th-century church below. Deeper still, the rough walls of the Roman house and the enigmatic symbols of the Mithraic temple offer glimpses into a more distant past.

As you descend, the sounds of the modern city fade away. The air grows cooler, damper. The weight of history presses in from all sides. It's easy, in such an atmosphere, to believe in phantom bells and ancient mysteries.

· · ·

Some visitors claim to have heard the bells themselves. They speak of a sound unlike any church bell they've heard before - deeper, more resonant, with a quality that seems to bypass the ears and vibrate directly in the bones. Others describe not so much a sound as a feeling, a sense of something vast and ancient stirring far below.

Skeptics, of course, have their own explanations. They point to the acoustics of the ancient structures, which can play tricks on the ears. Perhaps, they suggest, the fabled bells are nothing more than the echo of real bells from nearby churches, distorted by the underground chambers. Or maybe it's the rumble of the metro, running deep beneath the city streets, transformed by expectation into something more mysterious.

But such rational explanations do little to diminish the power of the legend. In a city as old as Rome, where every stone seems to hold a story, the line between fact and folklore often blurs. The phantom bells of San Clemente are as much a part of the basilica's history as its physical structure.

The legend has evolved over time, adapting to reflect the changing fears and hopes of each era. During the turbulent Middle Ages, the bells were said to ring as a warning of impending disaster. In the Renaissance, they became a symbol of hidden knowledge, rung by the ghosts of ancient sages. During World War II, some claimed the bells tolled to mark the souls of the fallen.

Today, the phantom bells continue to inspire. Urban explorers and ghost hunters flock to San Clemente, hoping to capture evidence of the supernatural. Composers have written pieces meant to replicate the elusive tones of the spectral chimes. Writers weave the legend into tales of mystery and suspense.

But perhaps the true power of the phantom bells lies not in their sound, but in their silence. For every visitor who claims to have heard them, thousands more strain their ears in vain. The bells, it seems, choose their audience carefully.

This selective silence adds another layer to the mystery. Why do some hear the bells while others don't? Is it a matter of belief, of openness to the supernatural? Or is it something deeper, a connection to the layers of history that lie beneath our feet?

·　·　·

The phantom bells of San Clemente serve as a reminder that Rome is a city where the boundaries between past and present, sacred and profane, seen and unseen, are remarkably thin. They challenge us to listen more closely, not just with our ears but with our imaginations, to the whispers of the past that surround us.

As night falls over Rome and the streets grow quiet, one might find themselves drawn to the ancient walls of San Clemente. Standing in its shadow, listening intently, you might hear nothing more than the distant hum of traffic or the call of a night bird. Or you might, if you're very lucky, catch the faint, impossible toll of bells that haven't rung in centuries.

Whether the phantom bells of San Clemente are real or merely a compelling legend, their story speaks to something deep in the human psyche. We are drawn to mysteries, to the idea that there are still secrets to be uncovered, even in a city as well-explored as Rome. The bells remind us that history is not a dead thing, confined to books and museums, but a living force that continues to shape our world in ways we might not always understand.

.   .   .

In the end, perhaps it doesn't matter whether the bells truly ring or not. Their legend has become a part of San Clemente's story, as integral to the basilica's identity as its ancient stones and precious artworks. They represent the persistence of the past, the layers of belief and culture that have shaped Rome over the millennia.

So the next time you find yourself in Rome, consider paying a visit to San Clemente. Descend through its layers, feel the weight of history around you. And as you stand in the cool darkness of its lowest level, among the remnants of faiths long past, listen carefully. You may not hear the phantom bells - but in the silence, you might just catch an echo of Rome's enduring mystery.

29

THE RESTLESS SPIRIT OF PALAZZO MASSIMO

Palazzo Massimo alle Colonne stands as a silent sentinel on the bustling Corso Vittorio Emanuele II, its Renaissance façade giving little hint of the secrets it holds within. But as night falls and the streets grow quiet, whispers of an centuries-old tragedy echo through its halls. For it's said that the palazzo is home to one of Rome's most enduring ghosts: the spirit of Costanza Conti, a young noblewoman whose life was cut tragically short in the 17th century.

The story of Costanza and her haunting is intertwined with the history of the Massimo family, one of Rome's oldest and most illustrious noble houses. The palazzo itself was built in the 16th century on the ruins of an ancient Roman theater, a fitting metaphor for the layers of drama that would unfold within its walls.

Costanza's tale begins in the early 1600s. Born into nobility, she was a vivacious young woman known for her beauty and charm. She caught the eye of a scion of the Massimo family, and their engagement was the talk of Roman high society. The future seemed bright for Costanza, full of promise and joy.

But fate had other plans. On the day of her wedding, as she prepared to walk down the aisle, Costanza suddenly fell ill. Some accounts speak of a fever that struck without warning, others of a mysterious malady that left doctors baffled. Whatever the cause, the result was the same: Costanza died before she could say her vows, her white wedding dress becoming her burial shroud.

The Massimo family was devastated. Costanza was laid to rest in the family chapel, and a pall of grief settled over the palazzo. But for Costanza, it seems, death was not the end of her story.

·   ·   ·

Soon after her funeral, strange occurrences began to be reported in the palazzo. Servants spoke of hearing music and laughter late at night, as if a grand ball was taking place in empty rooms. Others claimed to have seen a figure in a white dress gliding through the halls, always vanishing when approached.

As the years passed, the sightings became more frequent and more detailed. The ghost, for there was no doubt now that it was a ghost, was identified as Costanza herself. She appeared as she had on her wedding day: young, beautiful, and clad in her pristine white gown. But her expression was one of profound sadness, her eyes searching for something she could never find.

One of the most famous encounters with Costanza's ghost occurred in the 18th century. A young nobleman, staying at the palazzo as a guest of the Massimo family, awoke in the middle of the night to find his room filled with an unearthly light. There, at the foot of his bed, stood Costanza. She reached out to him, her lips moving as if to speak, but no sound emerged. When the terrified man cried out, she vanished, leaving behind only the lingering scent of lilies - the flowers that had adorned her on her wedding day.

· · ·

This encounter set the pattern for many that would follow. Costanza's ghost seemed drawn to the living, particularly to young men who resembled her lost love. She would appear to them, silent and sorrowful, before fading away. Some interpreted these visitations as a warning, others as a plea for help.

The Massimo family, for their part, came to accept Costanza's ghost as a part of their heritage. They spoke of her with a mixture of fear and affection, seeing her presence as a sign of her enduring connection to the family she had almost joined in life. Some even claimed that seeing Costanza's ghost was a sign of good fortune, a blessing from beyond the grave.

But not all of Costanza's appearances were benign. There were whispers of darker encounters, of nights when her sorrow turned to rage. Furniture would be found overturned, objects hurled across rooms by unseen hands. On the anniversary of her death, it was said, her cries could be heard echoing through the palazzo, a heart-wrenching lament for a life and love cut short.

These more violent manifestations led some to speculate that there was more to Costanza's death than a simple illness. Rumors began to circulate that she had been poisoned, perhaps by a rival for her fiancé's affections or by someone who stood to gain from preventing the marriage. Her ghost's restlessness was seen as evidence of a life ended by treachery rather than natural causes.

Others saw Costanza's haunting as a reflection of unfinished business. In an era when marriage was often more about alliances than affection, Costanza and her fiancé had been a rare love match. Her ghost, some said, was not just mourning her own death, but the future she had been denied - a future of love, family, and happiness.

As the centuries passed, the legend of Costanza's ghost grew and evolved. Each generation added its own encounters and interpretations to the story. During the Napoleonic occupation of Rome, French soldiers billeted in the palazzo reported seeing a woman in white who led them through secret passages to safety. In the turbulent days of Italian unification, politicians meeting in secret at the palazzo claimed that Costanza's ghost appeared to warn them of impending danger.

The 20th century brought new perspectives to the haunting. Psychical researchers and paranormal investigators flocked to the palazzo, armed with cameras and electronic equipment. While some claimed to have captured evidence of supernatural activity, others left disappointed. The ghost of Costanza, it seemed, was not interested in performing for scientific instruments.

Today, the Palazzo Massimo alle Colonne stands as a testament to Rome's enduring ability to blend the past and present. Parts of the building have been converted into apartments and offices, while others remain in the hands of the Massimo family. Tourists pass by its façade every day, most unaware of the centuries of history and legend contained within its walls.

But for those who know the story, the palazzo holds a special allure. Ghost tours of Rome often stop outside, regaling visitors with the tale of Costanza and her eternal dance between this world and the next. Some claim to have seen a white figure in one of the upper windows, or to have felt a sudden chill as they pass by the building late at night.

The story of Costanza's ghost touches on universal themes that resonate across cultures and centuries. It speaks to our fear of death and our hope for something beyond it. It reflects our fascination with tragic love stories and our desire to believe that true love can transcend even the grave. And it taps into our enduring belief that the past is never truly gone, that the echoes of history continue to reverberate in the present.

For the Massimo family, Costanza's ghost has become a kind of immortal guardian. Her presence, whether real or imagined, serves as a link to their illustrious past and a reminder of the enduring nature of their lineage. Some family members speak of feeling a protective presence in times of trouble, attributing it to the watchful spirit of the bride who never was.

Skeptics, of course, have their own explanations for the Costanza legend. They point to the power of suggestion, the way stories can shape our perceptions and experiences. The palazzo's long history and imposing architecture create an atmosphere ripe for ghostly imaginings. What one person interprets as a supernatural encounter, another might see as a trick of light and shadow, a half-remembered dream, or the product of an overactive imagination fueled by too many ghost stories.

.   .   .

Yet even for skeptics, the legend of Costanza holds a certain power. It's a reminder of the way stories shape our understanding of place and history. The palazzo is not just a building, but a repository of memories, hopes, and fears accumulated over centuries. Costanza's ghost, whether real or fictional, has become an integral part of that accumulated history.

As night falls over Rome and the lights of the city flicker to life, Palazzo Massimo alle Colonne stands in silent dignity. Behind its windows, shadows move in ways that might be the trick of the light or might be something more. And perhaps, if you listen closely, you might hear the faint rustle of a wedding dress, the echo of music from a ball that never was, the whisper of a love story that refuses to end.

The ghost of Costanza Conti, like so many of Rome's legends, blurs the line between history and myth, between the tangible world of stone and mortar and the intangible realm of spirit and memory. Her story reminds us that in Rome, the past is never far away. It lingers in ancient ruins and Renaissance palazzos, in whispered legends and enduring mysteries. And sometimes, just sometimes, it might appear before us in the form of a bride who never was, eternally seeking the happiness that was snatched away on what should have been the happiest day of her life.

30

UNRAVELING THE MYSTERY OF
POPE JOAN

In the annals of papal history, few stories are as controversial and captivating as that of Pope Joan. The tale of a woman who allegedly ascended to the highest seat of the Catholic Church, disguised as a man, only to be discovered after giving birth during a procession, has fascinated and divided people for centuries. It's a story that challenges our understanding of medieval history, gender roles, and the very foundations of one of the world's oldest institutions.

The legend, as it's most commonly told, unfolds in the mid-9th century. A brilliant and ambitious young woman, often referred to as Joan or Johanna, yearns for knowledge in a world where education is largely denied to her sex.

Disguising herself as a man, she enters a monastery, where her intellect and piety quickly set her apart. Rising through the ecclesiastical ranks, she eventually reaches Rome, where her reputation for wisdom and virtue leads to her election as pope.

For two and a half years, according to the story, Pope Joan rules the Church with skill and compassion. Her true identity remains a secret, known to none. But fate has other plans. During a procession through the streets of Rome, Joan suddenly goes into labor. The shock of a pope giving birth in public causes a scandal of unprecedented proportions. In some versions of the tale, Joan and her child are immediately killed by the outraged populace. In others, she is imprisoned or exiled, never to be heard from again.

The story of Pope Joan first appeared in chronicles in the 13th century, several hundred years after her supposed reign. It quickly captured the imagination of medieval Europe, spreading through manuscripts, artwork, and oral tradition. The tale was embellished and expanded upon over time, with different versions offering conflicting details about Joan's origins, the length of her papacy, and her ultimate fate.

.   .   .

One of the most intriguing aspects of the Pope Joan legend is how it intersects with verifiable historical events. The period in which she supposedly reigned, between the papacies of Leo IV and Benedict III, was indeed a tumultuous time for the Church. The papal throne was subject to political maneuvering and corruption, with rival factions vying for control. Could a woman have slipped into power amidst this chaos?

Proponents of the legend point to several pieces of evidence to support its veracity. They note the existence of a "Vicus Papissa" or "Street of the Female Pope" in medieval Rome, and the long-standing tradition of having newly elected popes sit in a chair with a hole in the seat, allegedly to verify their male anatomy. Some even claim that certain medieval papal coins and seals bear the image of a woman, possibly Joan herself.

However, historians and the Catholic Church vehemently deny the possibility of a female pope. They argue that the continuous records of papal succession leave no room for Joan's reign. The chair with the hole, they explain, was likely a birthing chair repurposed for ceremonial use. As for the "Street of the Female Pope," it may have been named after a notable Roman woman or been a corruption of a similar-sounding name.

· · ·

Despite these rebuttals, the legend of Pope Joan has persisted, evolving to reflect the concerns and attitudes of different eras. During the Protestant Reformation, the story was seized upon as evidence of the corruption and fallibility of the Catholic Church. In the 19th and 20th centuries, as women began to challenge traditional gender roles, Joan became a symbol of female empowerment and the struggle against patriarchal institutions.

The enduring fascination with Pope Joan speaks to deeper truths about human nature and society. It taps into our love of secret identities and stories of exceptional individuals defying societal norms. Joan's rise to power, achieved through intellect and merit rather than birth or gender, resonates with modern ideals of equality and meritocracy.

Moreover, the legend highlights the complex relationship between gender and power throughout history. Joan's need to disguise herself as a man to access education and authority reflects the real limitations placed on women in medieval society. That such a deception could supposedly be maintained at the highest levels of the Church raises questions about the nature of gender identity and the arbitrary nature of many gender-based restrictions.

. . .

The story also serves as a cautionary tale about the dangers of deception and the consequences of challenging established order. In most versions of the legend, Joan's reign ends in tragedy, suggesting that there are limits to how far one can transgress societal norms without facing severe repercussions.

For the Catholic Church, the legend of Pope Joan has long been a thorn in its side. The very idea of a woman ascending to the papacy challenges fundamental doctrines about the male-only priesthood and papal infallibility. Over the centuries, Church authorities have gone to great lengths to debunk the story, presenting historical evidence to refute its possibility.

Yet even as historians dismiss the literal truth of the Pope Joan story, many acknowledge its significance as a cultural phenomenon. The legend has inspired countless works of art, literature, and film. It has been the subject of scholarly debates and popular speculation. In many ways, Pope Joan has become larger than life, a figure who exists in the realm of myth and symbol rather than historical fact.

. . .

The story continues to evolve in the modern era. Some feminist scholars have reinterpreted Joan not as a woman disguised as a man, but as a transgender individual, viewing the legend through the lens of gender identity and expression. Others see in Joan a reflection of the many women throughout history whose contributions have been erased or attributed to men.

As with many legends, the "truth" of Pope Joan may be less important than what the story reveals about the society that created and perpetuated it. It speaks to medieval anxieties about women in power, to the Catholic Church's complex relationship with gender, and to the enduring human fascination with stories of secret identities and spectacular falls from grace.

Walking through the streets of Rome today, one might still encounter echoes of the Pope Joan legend. Though the "Vicus Papissa" no longer exists, tour guides often point out sites associated with the story. In the Basilica of San Clemente, a medieval fresco depicts a figure some believe to be Joan. And in countless souvenir shops, one can find images of the female pope, her story reduced to a kitschy postcard or refrigerator magnet.

.   .   .

But perhaps the true legacy of Pope Joan lies not in physical artifacts or historical debates, but in the questions her story continues to provoke. What does it mean to be qualified to lead? How do societal expectations shape our understanding of gender and power? And how do legends and myths influence our perception of history and truth?

As the sun sets over Rome and the ancient stones of the city glow in the fading light, one might pause to consider the story of Pope Joan. In the narrow alleys and grand piazzas, in the shadows of churches and palaces, her legend lives on - a reminder that history is not always what it seems, and that the most enduring stories are often those that challenge our assumptions and ignite our imaginations.

Whether Pope Joan ever truly existed or not, her story has become an integral part of Rome's vast tapestry of legends and mysteries. It stands as a testament to the power of narrative, to the enduring human desire to challenge the status quo, and to the complex interplay between fact and fiction that shapes our understanding of the past. In the end, perhaps that is Pope Joan's true legacy - not as a historical figure, but as a symbol of the stories we tell ourselves about power, gender, and the endless possibilities of human potential.

31

BERNINI'S OBELISK

Nestled in the Piazza della Minerva, just a stone's throw from the Pantheon, stands one of Rome's most curious monuments. A small Egyptian obelisk, ancient and inscrutable, balances improbably on the back of a marble elephant. This is the Elephant Obelisk, a creation of the baroque master Gian Lorenzo Bernini, and a monument that has puzzled and fascinated Romans and visitors alike for over three centuries.

At first glance, the obelisk might seem whimsical, even playful. The elephant, with its trunk curled upwards and a blanket draped over its back, appears to bear its ancient burden with a sense of joy. But look closer, and you'll find layers of symbolism, hidden messages, and enduring mysteries that have made this small monument a subject of speculation and study for generations.

The story of the Elephant Obelisk begins in 1665, when workers digging in the garden of the nearby Dominican monastery uncovered a small Egyptian obelisk. Such discoveries were not uncommon in Rome, where the layers of history often yielded unexpected treasures. This particular obelisk, dating back to the 6th century BCE, had once stood in the Temple of Isis in ancient Egypt before being brought to Rome during the imperial era.

Pope Alexander VII, a great patron of the arts and a believer in the power of public monuments to shape civic life, saw an opportunity. He commissioned Bernini, already famous for his sculptures and architectural works throughout Rome, to create a monument that would incorporate the obelisk.

Bernini's design was both innovative and deeply symbolic. The elephant, an animal rarely seen in European art of the time, was chosen for its association with wisdom, strength, and piety in both Christian and Egyptian traditions. The obelisk itself, with its ancient hieroglyphs, represented hidden knowledge and the wisdom of ages past.

But it's in the details of the design that the true mysteries of the Elephant Obelisk begin to emerge. Bernini incorporated a number of curious elements that have fueled speculation about hidden meanings and secret messages for centuries.

The elephant's stance, for instance, has been a subject of much debate. Its left leg is raised slightly, as if it's about to take a step. Some have interpreted this as a symbol of wisdom in motion, the idea that true knowledge is always progressing. Others see it as a reference to the philosophical concept of "learned ignorance" - the understanding that the more we know, the more we realize how much we don't know.

The elephant's trunk, curled upwards, has also been the subject of various interpretations. Some see it as a gesture of triumph or joy, while others interpret it as a symbol of the search for higher knowledge. There are even those who claim that the curve of the trunk, when viewed from certain angles, forms a perfect logarithmic spiral - a shape found throughout nature and associated with divine proportion.

Perhaps the most intriguing element of the monument is the inscription on its base: "SAPIENTIS AEGYPTI INSCULPTAS OBELISCO FIGURAS AB ELEPHANTO BELLUARUM FORTISSIMA GESTARI QUISQUIS HIC VIDES DOCUMENTUM INTELLIGE ROBUSTAE MENTIS ESSE SOLIDAM SAPIENTIAM SUSTINERE." This roughly translates to: "Whoever you are who sees here the figures of Egyptian wisdom engraved on the obelisk carried by an elephant, the strongest of beasts, understand that it is a symbol that a strong mind is needed to support solid wisdom."

This inscription has been analyzed and reinterpreted countless times over the centuries. Some see it as a straightforward explanation of the monument's symbolism. Others believe it contains hidden messages, perhaps even clues to esoteric knowledge that Bernini and his patrons wanted to preserve.

The placement of the monument adds another layer to its mystery. It stands in the Piazza della Minerva, named for the ancient Roman goddess of wisdom, whose temple once stood nearby. The obelisk faces the church of Santa Maria sopra Minerva, creating a dialogue between pagan and Christian symbols of wisdom and faith.

Over the years, the Elephant Obelisk has accrued a number of legends and stories. Some say that on certain nights, when the moon is full and the piazza is empty, the elephant comes to life and walks around the square, the obelisk on its back glowing with an otherworldly light. Others claim that if you stand in just the right spot at just the right time, the shadows cast by the monument reveal hidden messages or symbols.

These tales, while fanciful, speak to the enduring fascination that the Elephant Obelisk holds for those who encounter it. It's a monument that seems to invite speculation and interpretation, a puzzle waiting to be solved.

In more recent times, scholars and art historians have applied modern techniques to try to unravel the obelisk's secrets. Detailed scans and measurements have revealed subtle asymmetries in the elephant's design, leading some to speculate that Bernini intentionally incorporated these imperfections as part of the monument's hidden meaning.

. . .

Others have focused on the hieroglyphs on the obelisk itself. While many of the symbols were misunderstood or misinterpreted in Bernini's time, modern Egyptology has allowed for more accurate translations. The inscriptions speak of ancient pharaohs and long-forgotten rituals, adding another layer of mystery to the monument.

The Elephant Obelisk has also been the subject of numerous restoration efforts over the centuries. Each time scaffolding goes up around the monument, rumors swirl about what might be discovered. Will hidden compartments be found within the elephant's body? Are there secret inscriptions invisible to the naked eye? While these restorations have yet to yield any earth-shattering discoveries, they serve to keep the mystery of the obelisk alive in the public imagination.

For many Romans, the Elephant Obelisk is more than just a curiosity or a tourist attraction. It's become a beloved symbol of their city's endless capacity to surprise and delight. Locals often use it as a meeting point, arranging to gather "at the elephant" before heading off to explore the nearby sights or enjoy a coffee in one of the piazza's cafes.

. . .

The monument has also inspired countless artists, writers, and filmmakers over the years. It's appeared in novels as a meeting place for secret societies, in films as a backdrop for clandestine exchanges, and in paintings that seek to capture its enigmatic charm. Each new interpretation adds to the rich tapestry of myth and meaning that surrounds the obelisk.

As day turns to night in Rome and the lights come up in the Piazza della Minerva, the Elephant Obelisk takes on a different character. Shadows play across its surface, the marble elephant seeming to shift and move in the flickering light. It's in these moments that one can almost believe the old stories about hidden messages and secret knowledge.

Whether you see the Elephant Obelisk as a masterpiece of baroque art, a repository of ancient wisdom, or simply a charming curiosity, there's no denying its power to captivate and intrigue. It stands as a testament to Rome's layered history, a bridge between ancient Egypt and the baroque splendor of the 17th century, and a continuing source of mystery and wonder.

· · ·

In a city filled with monumental works of art and architecture, the Elephant Obelisk holds its own, not through size or grandeur, but through its ability to spark the imagination. It reminds us that sometimes the greatest mysteries come in small packages, and that even after centuries of study and speculation, there are still secrets waiting to be uncovered in the eternal city.

As you stand before the Elephant Obelisk, watching the play of light and shadow across its ancient stones, you might find yourself drawn into the centuries-old game of interpretation and speculation. What messages might be hidden in its graceful curves and enigmatic inscriptions? What secrets does the elephant keep? In the end, perhaps the true magic of the Elephant Obelisk lies not in any hidden knowledge it might contain, but in its ability to keep us wondering, to keep us looking closer, and to remind us that in Rome, mystery and history are always intertwined.

32

THE ENIGMA OF THE VATICAN LIBRARY

Behind the imposing walls of Vatican City lies a treasure trove of knowledge that has fascinated scholars, conspiracy theorists, and adventure seekers for centuries. The Vatican Library, established in 1475 by Pope Sixtus IV, is not just a repository of books and manuscripts; it's a labyrinth of secrets, a guardian of hidden knowledge, and a source of endless speculation.

The library's origins stretch back even further than its official founding date. The Catholic Church had been collecting texts since its earliest days, accumulating a vast array of writings on theology, philosophy, and history. But it was Pope Nicholas V in the mid-15th century who first conceived of a public library for the "common convenience of the learned." His vision was realized by Sixtus

IV, who formally established the library and appointed the first Vatican Librarian.

From its inception, the Vatican Library was more than just a collection of religious texts. The Church's global reach and diplomatic connections allowed it to amass an unparalleled collection of works from around the world. Ancient Greek and Roman manuscripts, Arabic scientific texts, and even documents from as far away as China found their way onto the library's shelves.

But it's not just the breadth of the collection that has sparked imaginations; it's what might be hidden within it. For centuries, rumors have circulated about secret vaults and restricted sections housing texts too dangerous or controversial for public view. Some speak of ancient prophecies that could shake the foundations of faith. Others whisper about scientific treatises far ahead of their time, suppressed to maintain the Church's worldview.

One persistent legend speaks of a hidden archive of documents related to the Church's interactions with extraterrestrial beings. According to this tale, the Vatican has been in contact with alien civilizations for centuries, with the evidence carefully concealed within the library's most secure vaults. While most scholars dismiss such claims as fantasy, they've become a staple of conspiracy theories and speculative fiction.

Another enduring mystery surrounds the fate of the Library of Alexandria's lost works. When the great library of the ancient world was destroyed, countless irreplaceable texts were thought to be lost forever. But some believe that a significant portion of the collection was secretly salvaged and eventually made its way to the Vatican. The idea that the lost wisdom of antiquity might be gathering dust in some forgotten corner of the Vatican Library is tantalizing to historians and treasure hunters alike.

The library's restricted access policies have only fueled speculation about what might be hidden within. For centuries, only a select few scholars were granted permission to study its rarest texts, and even today, access is tightly controlled. Researchers must demonstrate a genuine academic need and undergo a rigorous vetting process before being allowed into the inner sanctum of the library.

. . .

This air of secrecy extends to the physical space of the library itself. Visitors often describe a sense of entering another world as they pass through its doors. The main reading room, with its frescoed ceilings and rows of ancient tomes, feels more like a temple of knowledge than a mere library. But it's the areas off-limits to the public that really set imaginations racing. What treasures or terrible secrets might be hiding in those restricted stacks and climate-controlled vaults?

One of the most intriguing aspects of the Vatican Library is its collection of coded or encrypted texts. The Voynich Manuscript, a book written in an unknown script and filled with bizarre illustrations, is perhaps the most famous of these. But there are countless other documents in the library's collection that have yet to be fully deciphered. Some believe these texts contain alchemical formulas, magical incantations, or prophecies of future events.

The library has also been at the center of numerous historical controversies. During the Reformation, it was accused of hoarding texts that contradicted Catholic doctrine. In the Galileo affair, the library played a crucial role in the suppression of heliocentric theory. More recently, scholars have debated whether the library might contain evidence of the Church's complicity in various historical atrocities.

But for all the rumors and speculation, the reality of the Vatican Library is in many ways more fascinating than the myths. Its collection includes some of the oldest surviving manuscripts of the Bible, irreplaceable works of classical literature, and scientific texts that shaped our understanding of the world. The library's archives contain correspondence from some of history's most significant figures, offering unparalleled insights into the past.

In recent years, the Vatican has made efforts to demystify the library and make its contents more accessible. A massive digitization project is underway, with the goal of preserving fragile manuscripts and making them available to scholars around the world. This openness, however, has done little to quell the rumors of hidden vaults and secret texts.

One persistent legend speaks of a mysterious room known as the "Chamber of Tears." According to this tale, deep within the library lies a chamber filled with texts so heretical or dangerous that anyone who reads them is driven to weep uncontrollably. While librarians dismiss this as pure fiction, the story continues to captivate those who believe the Vatican is hiding world-changing secrets.

Another area of speculation concerns the library's collection of magical and occult texts. Despite the Church's official stance against magic and the occult, the Vatican Library is known to house an extensive collection of grimoires, spell books, and works on demonology. Some claim that these books are kept not just for academic study, but as part of the Church's ongoing battle against dark forces.

The library's vast collection of astronomical texts and observations has also fueled conspiracy theories. Some believe that the Vatican has been tracking celestial phenomena for centuries, accumulating knowledge about cosmic events and their impact on Earth. This has led to speculation about whether the library contains predictions of future cataclysms or evidence of past ones that have been hidden from the public.

Even the library's architecture is a source of mystery. Visitors have reported strange acoustic phenomena, where whispers from one end of a room can be clearly heard at the other. Some believe these are intentional design features, allowing for secret communications or eavesdropping. Others see them as evidence of the library's mystical nature, as if the very walls are alive with the knowledge contained within.

The Vatican Library's role in global politics has been another source of intrigue. As a center of learning and a repository of historical documents, it has often found itself at the crossroads of world events. During World War II, for instance, there were rumors that the library was used to hide Jewish refugees and to safeguard cultural treasures from Nazi looting. Some even speculate that critical wartime intelligence was passed through the library's networks of scholars and clergy.

In the digital age, new mysteries have emerged. The Vatican's efforts to digitize its collection have been accompanied by stringent cybersecurity measures. This has led to speculation about what digital secrets the library might be protecting. Are there encrypted files that even the most advanced computers can't crack? Or databases of knowledge too sensitive to risk falling into the wrong hands?

Despite all the mysteries and legends, the true value of the Vatican Library lies not in hidden secrets but in its role as a preserver of human knowledge and culture. Its collection spans the breadth of human experience, from ancient religious texts to modern scientific papers. It stands as a testament to the enduring power of the written word and humanity's quest for understanding.

As night falls over Rome and the lights dim in the Vatican's windows, one can imagine the library's vast halls standing silent and dark. But in that darkness, the accumulated wisdom of centuries waits patiently on countless shelves. What discoveries remain to be made among those ancient tomes? What insights into our past - and possibly our future - might be gleaned from their pages?

The mystery of the Vatican Library is not just about what might be hidden or forbidden. It's about the endless potential for discovery that lies within any great repository of knowledge. It's about the power of books and manuscripts to transport us across time and space, to challenge our understanding of the world, and to connect us with the thoughts and experiences of those who came before us.

In the end, perhaps the greatest secret of the Vatican Library is not any single text or artifact, but the very nature of knowledge itself - always growing, always changing, and always holding the potential to reshape our world in ways we can scarcely imagine. As long as its shelves stand filled with books and its vaults with manuscripts, the Vatican Library will continue to captivate our imaginations and fuel our quest for understanding.

33

THE DARK HISTORY OF CAMPO DE' FIORI

Campo de' Fiori, a bustling square in the heart of Rome, hides a grim past beneath its vibrant market stalls and cafe terraces. Today, it's a place where locals shop for fresh produce and tourists sip espresso, but in the 16th century, it was a stage for Rome's darkest spectacles. This was where accused witches and heretics met their fiery ends, their screams echoing off the surrounding buildings as flames consumed them.

The square's name, which translates to "Field of Flowers," belies its brutal history. In the 1500s, it was not flowers that bloomed here, but pyres. The Roman Inquisition, established in 1542 to combat the spread of Protestantism and root out heresy, turned Campo de' Fiori into its preferred site for public executions.

.   .   .

These were not swift affairs. An execution in Campo de' Fiori was an elaborate ritual, designed to strike fear into the hearts of would-be heretics and reaffirm the Church's authority. The condemned would be led through the streets, often forced to wear a sanbenito, a penitential garment painted with flames and devils. As they approached the square, the crowd's jeers would grow louder, mixing with the tolling of church bells.

In the center of the square, a pyre would be waiting. The accused would be given one last chance to repent. Some did, hoping for a quicker death by strangulation before the flames were lit. Others remained defiant to the end, refusing to renounce their beliefs even as the fire licked at their feet.

Among those who met their end in Campo de' Fiori were numerous women accused of witchcraft. The witch hunts that swept through Europe in the 16th and 17th centuries did not spare Rome. Women who were outsiders in their communities, those with knowledge of herbal medicine, or simply those who had run afoul of their neighbors could find themselves branded as witches.

.   .   .

One such woman was Gostanza da Libbiano, a midwife and healer from a small village near Pisa. Accused of witchcraft in 1594, she was brought to Rome for trial. Despite initially confessing under torture, Gostanza later recanted and maintained her innocence. Her fate was sealed when a local priest testified that he had seen her flying on a broomstick. On a crisp autumn morning, Gostanza was led to the pyre in Campo de' Fiori, her cries of innocence lost in the roar of the flames.

But it wasn't just accused witches who faced the fire in Campo de' Fiori. The square became the final destination for anyone deemed a threat to the established order. Jews forced to convert to Christianity who were caught practicing their ancestral faith in secret, known as marranos, often ended up here. So did Protestant sympathizers, freethinkers, and scientists whose ideas challenged Church doctrine.

Perhaps the most famous execution in Campo de' Fiori was that of Giordano Bruno on February 17, 1600. Bruno, a Dominican friar turned philosopher, had spent years traveling across Europe, expounding ideas that were radically ahead of his time. He proposed that the universe was infinite, containing countless worlds, and that the sun was just one star among many. These concepts, commonplace today, were considered dangerous heresy in Bruno's time.

After years of investigation, Bruno was found guilty of heresy on multiple counts. He was stripped of his priestly orders, excommunicated, and sentenced to death. On the day of his execution, Bruno was led to Campo de' Fiori. Legend has it that when he was offered a crucifix to kiss before the flames were lit, he turned his face away. As the fire consumed him, Bruno reportedly remained silent, his defiant gaze fixed on the sky he had dared to reimagine.

The executions in Campo de' Fiori were not just about punishing individuals; they were public spectacles designed to reinforce social and religious norms. Attending these events was often mandatory for Rome's citizens. Children were brought to witness the gruesome scenes, a harsh lesson in the consequences of defying authority.

The air in Campo de' Fiori on execution days was thick with more than just smoke. The smell of burning flesh mingled with the scent of herbs and spices sold in the market stalls that ringed the square. Vendors did brisk business, selling food and drink to the crowds that gathered to watch. It was a carnival atmosphere, with death as the main attraction.

Not all those sentenced to die in Campo de' Fiori were burned alive. Some were granted the relative mercy of strangulation before their bodies were consigned to the flames. Others were drawn and quartered, their dismembered bodies displayed as a warning to others. The methods might vary, but the message remained the same: deviation from the approved path would not be tolerated.

As the 16th century gave way to the 17th, the frequency of executions in Campo de' Fiori began to wane. The fervor of the Counter-Reformation gradually cooled, and the Roman Inquisition's influence diminished. The last execution for heresy in the square took place in 1720.

But the memory of those fiery spectacles lingered. For years after the executions stopped, locals claimed to hear phantom screams echoing across the square on quiet nights. Some reported seeing ghostly flames flickering in the spot where the pyres once stood. Whether these were genuine paranormal experiences or simply the product of guilty consciences, they kept the square's dark history alive in the public imagination.

.   .   .

Today, Campo de' Fiori bears little visible evidence of its gruesome past. The only hint is a stern-faced statue of Giordano Bruno, erected in 1889 on the very spot where he was burned. Bruno stands defiantly, his cowled face turned towards the Vatican, a silent rebuke to those who once condemned him.

The statue's installation was itself a controversial act. The Catholic Church, which had only recently lost its temporal power over Rome, opposed the monument. Its erection marked a turning point, a public acknowledgment of the injustices committed in the name of faith. Bruno, once reviled as a heretic, was now celebrated as a martyr for free thought.

As visitors stroll through Campo de' Fiori today, few realize they're walking on ground once soaked with the blood and ashes of the condemned. The cheerful market stalls and bustling cafes have long since replaced the scaffold and the pyre. But for those who know its history, the square remains a poignant reminder of humanity's capacity for both cruelty and resilience.

.   .   .

The story of the witch hunts and heretic burnings in Campo de' Fiori is more than just a grim chapter in Rome's history. It's a cautionary tale about the dangers of absolutism, the consequences of fear and ignorance, and the courage of those who dare to challenge prevailing beliefs. It reminds us that progress often comes at a terrible cost, paid by those who are ahead of their time.

In a twist of historical irony, many of the ideas that once led to execution in Campo de' Fiori are now commonly accepted. Bruno's concept of an infinite universe populated by countless worlds is borne out by modern astronomy. The healing practices that once branded women as witches are now studied as traditional medicine. The religious tolerance that was once punishable by death is now enshrined in law in many parts of the world.

As night falls over Campo de' Fiori and the last market vendors pack up their stalls, the square takes on a different character. The chatter of daytime crowds gives way to the laughter of evening revelers. But in the quieter corners, away from the bright lights of bars and restaurants, one might still feel a chill that has nothing to do with the evening air.

. . .

Perhaps it's just the weight of history, the echoes of centuries of human drama played out on these cobblestones. Or perhaps it's something more - the restless spirits of those who met their fiery ends here, still seeking justice or understanding. Either way, Campo de' Fiori stands as a complex monument to human nature, where the darkness of our past and the light of our potential for change coexist in uneasy balance.

The next time you find yourself in this lively Roman square, take a moment to look beyond the colorful market stalls and bustling cafes. Remember the flames that once lit up this place, not in celebration but in grim judgment. And consider how far we've come - and how far we still have to go - in our eternal struggle against ignorance, intolerance, and fear.